TELEPHONE DIPLOMACY
The Secret Talks Behind US-Soviet Détente During the Cold War, 1969-1977

Daniel S. Stackhouse, Jr., Ph.D.

CreateSpace Independent Publishing Platform
Copyright Daniel S. Stackhouse, Jr., 2014
All Rights Reserved.
ISBN-13: 978-1496029737
ISBN-10: 1496029739

For my daughter, Meera, who makes every day a sunny day.

Contents

Chapter 1

The Kissinger-Dobrynin Special Relationship

"Now, what it all gets down to is how two great powers, the two major powers in the world, are going to be able to talk about their differences rather than fight about them? You've got to set up a *relationship* [italics mine] on a personal basis or in some fashion whereby the differences can be discussed and the areas of self-interest can be discovered, worked out, and then increased. And that is what détente is all about."[1]
-Richard Nixon

How are international crises resolved? Unbeknownst to the public, many of them are handled by way of back channel negotiations (BCN). These secret, private communications between representatives of each side seek to find solutions to conflicts away from the heated rhetoric of politicians and the public.

One such back channel operated between US National Security Advisor and later Secretary of State Henry Kissinger and Soviet Ambassador to the US Anatoly Dobrynin during the 1970s. This era witnessed improved relations between the United States and the Soviet Union, known today as the period of "détente." One of détente's most noteworthy accomplishments occurred when US President Richard Nixon made a historic visit to Moscow in May, 1972, to sign the Strategic Arms Limitation Treaty (SALT I) with Leonid Brezhnev, General Secretary of the Communist Party of the Soviet Union. The treaty had two components: the Interim Agreement which froze offensive nuclear missiles at then-current levels for five years, and the Anti-Ballistic Missile Treaty (ABM) permanently limiting defensive nuclear weapons. Nixon and Brezhnev also concluded agreements on trade, sharing scientific and communication technology, as well as cultural exchanges. Several more US-Soviet summits followed throughout the decade.

Originating in the late 1960s, détente was an effort to relax tensions after more than twenty years of the Cold War between the United States and the Soviet Union, two nations with competing social systems – democratic capitalism and totalitarian communism, respectively. The overriding concern was that the two superpowers might allow their

---

[1] *Frost/Nixon – The Complete Interviews*, 400 min., Paradine Television Inc., 1977, DVD.

differences to spiral out of control and lead to a nuclear war. Several factors precipitated the change from confrontation to negotiation including the development of nuclear parity between the United States and the Soviet Union, the emergence of powerful economic rivals in Western Europe and Japan, as well as the birth of new nations in the developing world where both Washington and Moscow competed for influence.

However, by the end of the 1970s détente – the relaxing of tensions which had brought so much hope and progress to efforts of avoiding confrontation and even a potential nuclear war – was dead. While many believed that the immediate cause stemmed from the Soviet invasion of Afghanistan in 1979 and the subsequent withdrawal of a second treaty known as SALT II from Senate consideration, a deeper examination revealed fissures in the rapprochement almost from the very beginning. Accusations by both sides of violating agreed upon limits in nuclear weapons plagued the period. In addition, disagreements on the subjects of human rights and foreign interventions in the developing world further endangered progress.

The Americans used a French word, détente, for this thaw in the Cold War, while the Russians preferred *razryadka*. While both can be translated as "relaxing tensions," the difference in terms indicated a fundamental difference in understanding of what "relaxing tensions" actually meant. For the Americans, détente meant peace through arms control, trade, and various forms of scientific, technical, and cultural exchanges. However, it also included an anticipated change in Soviet behavior, both domestically in terms of respecting Western notions of human rights and internationally by refraining from interference in the affairs of newly formed nations in the developing world. For the Soviets, *razryadka* referred strictly to those subjects they considered appropriate topics of state-to-state relations: arms control to prevent nuclear war, trade, and earning respect as a co-equal superpower.

Despite these differences, there were numerous successes during détente's early period from 1969-1975. Accomplishments including the Interim Agreement and ABM Treaty, dramatically increasing emigration for Jews wishing to leave the Soviet Union, as well as ending American involvement in the Vietnam War and bringing about a ceasefire during the October, 1973 Arab-Israeli conflict attest to this.

Where progress was possible in US-Soviet relations, it was largely attributable to an empathetic relationship which developed between Kissinger and Dobrynin. Through their "backchannel" method of conducting diplomacy characterized by private meetings and telephone calls, Kissinger and Dobrynin crafted détente away from the State Department bureaucracy, the media, and the public. After their meetings face-to-face or over the phone, Kissinger provided memoranda to Nixon summarizing the discussions while Dobrynin did the same in telegrams to Brezhnev, Soviet Foreign Minister Andrei Gromyko, and other members of the Politburo in Moscow. However, transcripts of their telephone conversations provide an as-it-happened sense of their discussions. They also reveal that over time Kissinger and Dobrynin formed a relationship as well as established empathy and trust, thereby enabling them to make progress in US-Soviet relations in spite of vast ideological differences between their two countries. Thus the Kissinger-Dobrynin backchannel provides a valuable case study of the potential effectiveness of back channel negotiations for use in international diplomacy.

Kissinger's and Dobrynin's Views of Detente

Few individuals were more closely associated with US-Soviet détente than Henry Kissinger and Anatoly Dobrynin. Kissinger served as National Security Advisor and later also Secretary of State under Presidents Nixon and Ford from 1969-1977. Meanwhile Dobrynin held the post of Soviet Ambassador to the United States from 1962-1986, a period spanning all or part of the administrations of Presidents Kennedy, Johnson, Nixon, Ford, Carter, and Reagan.

Kissinger had a decidedly negative view of détente while in academia in the 1950s and 1960s. According to Steven F. Hayward, a scholar at the conservative Pacific Research Institute for Public Policy in San Francisco, in the 1950s when Kissinger was a professor at Harvard he had warned that the Soviet Union would use "détente and 'peace offensives'" in order to "divide and weaken domestic opposition in the West."[2] Then in 1965 he added that for the Soviets "'peaceful coexistence…is justified primarily as a tactical device to overthrow the West at minimum risk.'"[3]

After arriving in Washington, however, Kissinger modified his views of détente several times, according to Walter Isaacson.[4] One of Kissinger's biographers, Isaacson noted that in 1974 detente was "'the

---

[2] Steven F. Hayward, *The Age of Reagan – The Fall of the Old Liberal Order, 1964-1980* (Roseville, CA: Prima Publishing, Inc., 2001), 426.
[3] Ibid.
[4] Walter Isaacson, *Kissinger – A Biography* (New York: Simon & Schuster, 1992), 695.

search for a more productive relationship with the Soviet Union;'" in July, 1975, several months after the fall of Saigon to the North Vietnamese, it had morphed into "'a means to regulate a competitive relationship;'" and finally in 1976 it was simply "'designed to prevent Soviet expansion.'"[5] Clearly the changing definitions represented Kissinger's effort to scale back expectations as the US-Soviet relationship deteriorated.

Writing in 1982 after leaving office, Kissinger described détente as an adaptation to a time when Congress and the American people felt war-weary from Vietnam and less inclined to endorse military interventions and big defense budgets. He seemed to believe that relaxing tensions was a *necessity* based upon the realities of the 1970s:

> For the statesman in any event, a foreign policy issue does not present itself as a theory but as a series of realities. And the realities of Nixon's first term were stark. We had to end a war in Indochina in the midst of a virulent domestic assault on all the sinews of a strong foreign policy. It was followed by the impotence of the Presidency as a result of Watergate. Détente was not the cause of these conditions but one of the necessities for mastering them.[6]

Kissinger argued that despite what many conservatives believed, détente was not surrender to the Soviets in the Cold War, but an effort to wage the ideological struggle more efficiently and more in tune with national interests due to limited resources.[7] However, he also accused liberals of not assuming responsibility for driving America towards isolationism through their resistance to military involvement and military expenditures after Vietnam and Watergate.[8]

In general, Kissinger did not believe that Americans were prepared for détente. In 1994 he wrote, "[t]he combination of adversarial and cooperative conduct implicit in détente with the Soviet Union," did not conform to the American "black-and-white assumption" that the world was divided into friends and enemies.[9] The reality, he argued, was that

---

[5] Ibid., 695, 696.

[6] Henry Kissinger, *Years of Upheaval* (New York: Simon & Schuster, 1982), 235.

[7] Ibid., 236, 237.

[8] Ibid., 235, 236.

[9] Henry, Kissinger, *Diplomacy* (New York: Simon & Schuster, 1994), 741.

every country was "a combination of both."[10] Kissinger concluded that détente "challenged American exceptionalism and its imperative that policy be based on the affirmation of transcendent values."[11]

Like Kissinger, Anatoly Dobrynin had a distinguished academic background. His doctoral thesis on the Russo-Japanese War of 1905 and U.S. President Theodore Roosevelt led him to studying American diplomatic history.[12] After graduating from the Higher Diplomatic School, he then began his long career in the Soviet Foreign Ministry in the late 1940s.[13] In his 1995 memoirs Dobrynin identified détente for the Soviet Union as first and foremost a reaction to the danger of nuclear war. For Brezhnev and other high officials of the Communist Party, a nuclear confrontation was "utterly unacceptable."[14] Military costs, improving relations with Western Europe, preventing a US-Chinese alliance, and enhancing Brezhnev's profile in the Soviet Union were other motivating factors.[15]

On the other hand, Dobrynin believed that the American shift to détente resulted from a "painful reassessment of the political maxims of the Cold War."[16] US policy-makers faced Soviet missile parity and witnessed traditional allies including West Germany and France independently establishing improved relations with the Soviet Union.[17] Consequently, Washington felt compelled to abandon its policy of containment of the Soviet Union and take another tack. Dobrynin also noted "social and economic problems" which had been "seriously aggravated by the national gamble in Vietnam," causing the US to realize it could no longer pay for both "guns" and "butter" – military spending to wage the Cold War and social spending to fund President Lyndon Johnson's Great Society programs from the 1960s.[18]

Kissinger described detente as a practical necessity due to political, economic, and social changes in America, but not as surrender in the Cold

---

[10] Ibid.

[11] Ibid., 742.

[12] Anatoly Dobrynin, *In Confidence – Moscow's Ambassador to America's Six Cold War Presidents* (New York: Times Books, 1995), 19.

[13] Ibid., 18, 19.

[14] Ibid., 198.

[15] Ibid.

[16] Ibid., 199.

[17] Ibid.

[18] Ibid.

War. He sought to appease both the right and the left. By suggesting that détente was merely a change in tactics, Kissinger believed that he could appeal to conservatives who wanted to give no quarter to communism. Likewise, by reducing America's global commitments he hoped to convince liberals that there would be no more Vietnams.

Meanwhile, Dobrynin thought US acceptance of détente demonstrated America's acknowledgement that it could no longer rely on military strength to get its way in the world. For him, the American experience in Vietnam was a classic case of imperial overreach. He believed that the United States had realized that it could no longer block national liberation movements in the developing world, particularly when backed by the strengthened Soviet military. This interpretation implied American acceptance of the new status quo where the Soviet Union was an equal superpower and here to stay.

Thus Kissinger and Dobrynin were working from different premises while working to relax international tensions. Reconciling these differences as well as other distinctions between the wide-ranging American concept of détente and the Soviets' more limited notion of *razryadka* was the central task of the Kissinger-Dobrynin relationship. Although both continued to be self-interested advocates for their respective nations, they nevertheless forged a partnership which enabled them to overcome daunting challenges while negotiating arms control, human rights, and foreign interventions.

The Backchannel

According to Nixon, Kissinger had suggested having a private dialogue with Dobrynin even before they first met with the Soviet Ambassador on February 17, 1969, at the White House.[19] Nixon agreed, believing that such an arrangement might lead the ambassador to "be more forthcoming."[20] It began simply with Dobrynin arriving through the East Wing door of the White House for weekly lunches.[21] In 1979 Kissinger described the meetings as "a series of intimate exchanges that continued over eight years."[22] He added, "Increasingly, the most sensitive business

---

[19] Richard Nixon, *RN – The Memoirs of Richard Nixon* (New York: Grosset & Dunlap, 1978), 369.
[20] Ibid.
[21] Ibid.
[22] Henry Kissinger, *White House Years* (New York: Simon & Schuster, 1979), 138.

in US-Soviet relations came to be handled between Dobrynin and me."[23] The private meetings provided a forum to express points of view as well as test the reactions of each side to proposals. As Kissinger put it,

> We would, informally, clarify the basic purposes of our governments and when our talks gave hope of specific agreements, the subject was moved to conventional diplomatic channels. If formal negotiations there reached a deadlock, the Channel would open up again. We developed some procedures to avoid the sort of deadlock that can only be resolved as a test of strength.[24]

He described how both he and Dobrynin could raise an issue and get a response in a completely "non-committal" manner, thereby enabling them to "explore the terrain," and "avoid major roadblocks."[25] In 1994 Kissinger elaborated, explaining the circumstances surrounding the creation of what became known as "the backchannel" or simply "the channel":

> During his first term, Nixon had shifted much of the conduct of diplomacy into the White House, as he had announced he would during his presidential campaign. Once the Soviet leaders had grasped that Nixon would never delegate the key foreign policy decisions, a back-channel of direct contact developed between Soviet ambassador Anatoly Dobrynin and the white House. In this manner, the President and the top leadership in the Kremlin were able to deal directly with the most important issues.[26]

In 1995 Dobrynin described the backchannel as part of a "two-tier arrangement."[27] Although he continued to make "official contacts" with Secretary of State William Rogers, Dobrynin explained that Nixon also sought "to exchange views urgently and privately with the Soviet

---

[23] Ibid.

[24] Ibid., 139.

[25] Ibid.

[26] Kissinger, *Diplomacy*, 744.

[27] Dobrynin, *In Confidence*, 204.

leadership."[28] He called the backchannel with Kissinger "unprecedented in my experience and perhaps in the annals of diplomacy," due to its "extensive use."[29] Furthermore, its role "should not be underestimated."[30] He summed up its value in the following way:

> Looking back, I can say with certainty that had it not been for that channel, many key agreements on complicated and controversial issues would have never been reached, and dangerous tension would not have been eased... That was the beginning of our unique relations with the administration of Nixon and Kissinger. We were on many issues both opponents and partners in the preservation of peace.[31]

In 2007 Kissinger and Dobrynin elaborated on how the backchannel operated. Their meetings could be face-to-face or over the telephone. When they met in person, it was usually in the Map Room on the first floor of the White House, which Kissinger described as "sheltered from the outside world by verdant bushes, creating an atmosphere of seclusion, which removes the time pressures from the conversations – insofar as the pace of White House business allows it."[32] The purpose of their conversations could be to pass along communications from Nixon to Brezhnev and vice versa, or to break a deadlock in official negotiations between the traditional American and Soviet bureaucracies.[33] Dobrynin explained that previously he had conducted backchannels with members of the Kennedy and Johnson administrations, but only sporadically.[34] In contrast, the backchannel with Kissinger functioned as a direct conduit between the White House and the Kremlin on a permanent basis throughout Nixon's presidency.[35]

---

[28] Ibid.

[29] Ibid.

[30] Ibid., 205.

[31] Ibid., 206.

[32] Henry Kissinger, foreword to *Soviet-American Relations: The Détente Years, 1969-1972* (Washington, D.C.: United States Government Printing Office, 2007), xv.

[33] Ibid., xv, xvi.

[34] Anatoly Dobrynin, foreword to *Soviet-American Relations: The Détente Years, 1969-1972*, xxi.

[35] Ibid.

Secrecy was the defining characteristic of the backchannel. Its existence was only known to a relative few both in Washington and Moscow.[36] Furthermore, the conversations in person or over the phone were conducted without secretaries, translators, or note-takers. Afterwards Kissinger would compose a memorandum of conversation (memcon) for Nixon while Dobrynin would transmit a telegram to Moscow.[37] In 2007 these were collected in *Soviet-American Relations: The Détente Years, 1969-1972* by the Historian of the U.S. Department of State and the History and Records Department of the Russian Ministry of Foreign Affairs. However, Kissinger explained that in order to truly get a sense of how the backchannel functioned, it was also necessary to read the transcripts of his telephone conversations (telcons) with Dobrynin which were only printed in fragments for that collection.[38] This book provides a comprehensive study of those transcripts.

Kissinger and Dobrynin did not invent backchannels, but the Nixon administration probably surpassed any of its predecessors in the degree to which it relied upon this form of diplomacy. Kissinger also conducted backchannels with West German State Secretary Egon Bahr, US Ambassador to South Vietnam Ellsworth Bunker, US Ambassador William Porter at the Vietnam talks in Paris, and US Ambassador to Pakistan Joseph Farland.[39] This should not be surprising in light of Nixon's well-documented disdain for those whom he considered "east coast liberals" within the various federal government bureaucracies. Nixon provided a blunt explanation for why he and Kissinger were so secretive: ""[T]here have been more backchannel games played in this administration than any in history because we couldn't trust the God damned State Department[!]""[40] However, the backchannel with Dobrynin was probably unique in terms of the frequency and ease of its use due to the close proximity of the White House and the Soviet embassy in Washington, as well as the installation of a direct "hotline" between Kissinger's White House office and Dobrynin's embassy office.

---

[36] Mark J. Susser, preface to *Soviet-American Relations: The Détente Years, 1969-1972,* xxvii.

[37] Ibid.

[38] Kissinger, foreword to *Soviet-American Relations: The Détente Years, 1969-1972,* xv.

[39] Matthew Jones, "Between the Bear and the Dragon: Nixon, Kissinger and U.S. Foreign Policy in the Era of Détente," *English Historical Review* Vol. CXXIII, No. 504 (Oct. 2008): 1278.

[40] Ibid.

Backchannel diplomacy necessarily entailed secrecy, something for which the Nixon administration was often criticized. Liberals feared that Nixon and Kissinger were placing too much emphasis on geostrategic interests and balance of power theory while neglecting human rights concerns. Meanwhile, conservatives argued that the administration was endangering American national security by making arms control agreements which they believed favored the Soviet side. Additionally, Kissinger conceded that the administration was "cavalier" in its treatment of the regular civil service bureaucracy.[41] "Hell hath no fury like a bureaucrat scorned, and the Nixon White House compounded the problem by the insensitivity with which it overrode established procedure," he wrote.[42] In particular, Secretary of State William Rogers was cast aside. Such domestic pressures eventually combined with the conflicting American and Soviet views of relaxing tensions, ending détente and reigniting fears of nuclear war.

For some, back channel diplomacy is tainted due to its association with the scandal-ridden Nixon administration. Nevertheless, recent writings on back channel negotiations (BCN) have documented its numerous positive effects on resolving international conflicts. The private nature of BCN is essential for allowing representatives of hostile nations to begin negotiations amidst heated rhetoric from politicians and the public on both sides. Furthermore, the shared project of maintaining secrecy helps negotiators to establish a relationship based upon trust.

For example, Anthony Wanis-St. John, who focused on the Israeli-Palestinian dispute, claimed that all of the major signed agreements between Israel and the Palestinian Liberation Organization (PLO) resulted from the use of back channels "alone or in combination with front channels."[43] This included the 1993 Oslo Peace Accords where Israel and the PLO attained mutual recognition and the Palestinians acquired self-rule. Privacy was particularly necessary in cases such as this one where the two sides did not even recognize the legitimacy of the other. According to Wanis-St. John, back channels enabled leaders to isolate negotiations from "internal opponents (those most likely to oppose peace talks)," but this also caused difficulty "creating a broad consensus" to

---

[41] Kissinger, *Diplomacy*, 744.

[42] Ibid.

[43] Anthony Wanis-St. John, *Back Channel Negotiation: Secrecy in the Middle East Peace Process* (Syracuse, NY: Syracuse University Press, 2010), 5.

implement an agreement.[44] On the other hand traditional "front channel negotiations" often encountered problems attaining an agreement in the first place.[45] The answer, explained Wanis-St. John, was to "combine early but diminishing use of secrecy with gradually increasing public efforts to expand the central coalition on each side."[46]

Niall O'Dochartaigh contended that back channels resulted in the development of cooperative relationships between negotiators for the British government and the Irish Republican Army (IRA), helping lead to a historic 1998 settlement in Northern Ireland.[47] He argued that back channels "can contribute to a strong sense of joint enterprise and a common project" including keeping the negotiations secret.[48] This in turn helps lead to "a surprisingly robust negotiating relationship built on trust, continuity of personnel and a relationship of reciprocal exchange and limited compromise."[49]

Mikael Weissmann analyzed China's role in establishing back channels between North Korea and other countries like the United States who are concerned about Pyongyang's nuclear program.[50] He explained that "Personal networks and BCN [back channel negotiations] have been crucial ingredients for China's success in breaking escalation spirals, and in initiating cooperation, communication, and agreements, which has mitigated and de-escalated the conflict (at least temporarily)."[51] One method Beijing has used in negotiations is "informal pressure and signaling," including expressing support for United Nations sanctions whenever it believes that Pyongyang has exceeded proper boundaries.[52] Weismann concluded that from the time of the first trilateral meetings held in Beijing in 2003, Chinese involvement has been indispensable and "most probably" prevented military action against North Korea.[53]

---

[44] Ibid., 293.

[45] Ibid., 294.

[46] Ibid., 294-295.

[47] Niall O'Dochartaigh, "Together in the middle: Back-channel negotiation in the Irish peace process," *Journal of Peace Research* Vol. 48, No. 6 (November 2011): 770.

[48] Ibid., 768.

[49] Ibid.

[50] Mikael Weissmann, *The East Asian Peace: Conflict Prevention and Informal Peacebuilding* (Basingstoke: Palgrave Macmillan, 2012), 125.

[51] Ibid., 126.

[52] Ibid.

[53] Ibid., 124, 127.

The notion of using a secret "back door" or making "backroom deals" can understandably connote underhandedness and seem counter to expectations of honesty and openness in negotiations. However, similar to the cases cited above, the US-Soviet backchannel enabled Kissinger and Dobrynin to establish a relationship, and over time, fostered the empathy required to provide both with a sense of what was possible in negotiations and what would be "non-starters." Both understood the domestic political restraints that the other would face when it came time to "sell" an agreement.

As will be demonstrated in the following pages, the Kissinger-Dobrynin backchannel had four characteristics which help to explain its success: privacy, durability, ease and frequency of communication, and personality, the last of which is too often overlooked in history, which is after all the study of human beings and their actions individually or collectively.

The Telephone Transcripts

According to Dobrynin, during his face-to-face meetings with Kissinger there were neither interpreters nor secretaries present.[54] "This meant there was no official record of our meetings except what we kept ourselves," he added.[55] Nevertheless, he claimed there were never any disagreements about what had been said.[56] After those meetings, Kissinger typically prepared a memorandum of conversation (memcon) for Nixon while Dobrynin usually transmitted a telegram to Moscow. Obviously both would have had the opportunity to summarize their meetings in a way which they believed would please their respective superiors.

However, Kissinger explained that his secretaries transcribed "the overwhelming majority" of all his telephone conversations during his tenure as National Security Advisor and Secretary of State.[57] At first, the secretaries listened to the conversations on a "dead key" extension and drafted summaries, but eventually they began typing unedited, verbatim

---

[54] Dobrynin, *In Confidence*, 204.

[55] Ibid.

[56] Ibid.

[57] Henry Kissinger, *Crisis – The Anatomy of Two Major Foreign Policy Crises* (New York: Simon & Schuster, 2003), 1.

transcripts from shorthand notes or tape recordings.[58] It is not known what happened to the secretarial notes, but the tapes were immediately destroyed after being transcribed.[59] Kissinger described the purpose of the telephone conversation transcripts or telcons as "to enable me to follow up on promises made or understandings reached and to incorporate them into memoranda to the President or other records."[60] These private phone conversations with various leaders took place when Kissinger was at the White House, the State Department, San Clemente, Key Biscayne, Paris, New York, his home, and during airplane flights.[61]

However, most of the phone conversations between Kissinger and Dobrynin probably occurred when Kissinger was in his White House office and Dobrynin was in his office at the Soviet embassy in Washington. Dobrynin explained how secrecy was insured by the installation of a "hot line" in 1972:

> Later, as our contacts became more frequent and we met almost daily, the president ordered the installation of a direct and secure telephone line between the White House and the Soviet embassy for the exclusive use of Kissinger and me; we would just lift our receivers and talk, without dialing.[62]

It is not known if Dobrynin also recorded the phone conversations, so the telcons are probably the only such source available to historians of the period. These transcripts provide a previously unavailable, as-it-happened, and behind-the-scenes account of American-Soviet diplomacy during the extremely consequential years of the 1970s.

When Kissinger left office in 1977, he had the telcons placed temporarily at the estate of fellow Council on Foreign Relations member David Rockefeller before giving them to the Library of Congress.[63] They were not to be seen by the public until five years after Kissinger's death and even then only if the people with whom he was speaking were

---

[58] Nixon Presidential Materials Staff, "Henry A. Kissinger Telephone Conversation Transcripts (Telcons)," National Archives and Records Administration (May, 2004), 1.

[59] Ibid.

[60] Kissinger, *Crisis*, 1.

[61] Nixon Presidential Materials Staff, 1.

[62] Dobrynin, *In Confidence*, 205.

[63] Nixon Presidential Materials Staff, 2.

deceased or had given their approval.[64] According to Bruce P. Montgomery, associate professor and faculty director of archives at the University of Colorado at Boulder, Kissinger had first obtained an opinion from a State Department legal advisor (who served under him) that the transcripts were his personal property.[65] Kissinger's opponents argued that the transcripts from January, 1969, to August, 1974, were covered by the *Presidential Records and Materials Preservation Act* (1974), a statute passed specifically to enable Congress to acquire Nixon's tapes and records about the Watergate affair.[66] Meanwhile, State Department transcripts were said to be covered by the *Freedom of Information Act* (FOIA).[67]

In the late 1970s the Reporters Committee for Freedom of the Press fought to obtain access to the telcons in federal district court and the US court of appeals, both of which ruled that the transcripts were government records and should be released under FOIA.[68] Nevertheless, in 1980 the Supreme Court in *Kissinger v. Reporters Committee for Freedom of the Press* overturned the lower courts and claimed that the telcons were not part of the Executive branch and therefore not covered by FOIA.[69] However, the Court added that the *Federal Records Act* gave the Archivist of the United States as well as the Attorney General the power to retrieve records if they had not been removed properly.[70] Consequently the National Archives requested and Secretary of State Edmund Muskie agreed in 1980 to review the telcons at the Library of Congress so they could potentially be returned to the State department, but no further steps were taken.[71] For the next dozen years, Republican administrations under Ronald Reagan and then George H.W. Bush held the White House. Kissinger clearly benefitted from the presence of friendly administrations in his efforts to keep the telcons unavailable at the Library of Congress.

This period also coincided with when Kissinger was using memoranda of conversations based upon the transcripts to write his

---

[64] Ibid., 3.

[65] Bruce P. Montgomery, "*'Source Material'*: Sequestered from the Court of History: The Kissinger Transcripts," *Presidential Studies Quarterly* Vol. 34, No. 4 (Dec., 2004), 870.

[66] Ibid., 868.

[67] Ibid., 880, 881.

[68] Nixon Presidential Materials Staff, 3.

[69] Ibid.

[70] Ibid.

[71] Ibid.

memoirs from the Nixon era, *White House Years* (1979) and *Years of Upheaval* (1982).[72] The two volumes were "a work evidently written with great care to his [Kissinger's] place in history and to perpetuating his image as the consummate strategic thinker who executed sweeping and highly successful radical shifts in American foreign policy," wrote Montgomery.[73] However, if the transcripts were released they might "support an alternative assessment."[74] Nevertheless, Montgomery concluded that Kissinger did not seek to permanently keep the transcripts from the historical record. Based upon the terms of Kissinger's donation to the Library of Congress, "[h]e appeared more intent on sealing the documents until the extraordinary passions of the Watergate and Vietnam years had subsided and until after his death," wrote Montgomery.[75]

The telcons became known to the wider public during the Democratic administration of Bill Clinton, which was much more open to reviewing and releasing the transcripts which had long lain dormant at the Library of Congress. After Nixon's death in 1994, many of his presidential materials were released by the National Archives, including Kissinger's National Security office files which contained copies of a small portion of the transcripts.[76] Then in 1997 the State Department began publishing some of its copies of the telcons in its *Foreign Relations of the United States* (FRUS) series.[77] Repeated FOIA requests to release more of Nixon's documents by William Burr and others at the private National Security Archive housed at George Washington University led to the publication of *The Kissinger Transcripts: The Top Secret Talks with Beijing and Moscow* (1999).[78] However, this volume did not include any of the telephone conversation transcripts with Dobrynin, only a summary of one of their face-to-face meetings prepared by Kissinger for a memorandum.[79] Finally, in January, 2001, the National Security Archive threatened to go to court if the National Archives did not take steps to

---

[72] William Burr, "Omissions," available on the National Security Archive website at http://www.gwu.edu/~nsarchiv/nsa/publication/DOC_readers/kissinger/ommission.htm.

[73] Montgomery, 868.

[74] Ibid.

[75] Ibid., 874.

[76] Ibid., 887.

[77] Kissinger, *Crisis*, 1.

[78] Montgomery, 887.

[79] See William Burr, *The Kissinger Transcripts: The Top Secret Talks with Beijing and Moscow* (New York: The New Press, 1998), 43-46.

retrieve Kissinger's originals.[80] Having published the final volume of his memoirs, *Years of Renewal* in 1999, Kissinger may have been more inclined to release his papers since his version of history was now complete. Hence, State Department legal advisor William H. Taft IV convinced Kissinger to acquiesce and in August, 2001, release 10,000 pages of copies of the telephone conversation transcripts held at the Library of Congress from his tenure as Secretary of State, 1973-1977.[81] The following February he consented to the release of 20,000 more pages pertaining to his years as Nixon's National Security Advisor from 1969-1973.[82]

After review, the 20,000 pages of the Henry A. Kissinger Telephone Conversation Transcripts (Telcons) were released by the National Archives and Records Administration (NARA) on May 26, 2004.[83] That collection is housed at the Richard M. Nixon Presidential Library in Yorba Linda, California and covers January 21, 1969, to August 8, 1974, (from Nixon's first inauguration until his resignation) in thirty archival boxes.[84] Boxes 27 and 28 comprise the Anatoly Dobrynin file.[85] The State Department's collection is on-line and spans from August 9, 1974, until the end of the Ford Administration on January 20, 1977.[86] A few transcripts were withheld and some were redacted.[87]

---

[80] Montgomery, 889.
[81] Ibid.
[82] Ibid.
[83] Nixon Presidential Materials Staff, 1.
[84] Ibid., 1, 2.
[85] Ibid., 2.
[86] Ibid., 1.
[87] Ibid., 3, 4.

Chapter 2

Arms Control: A Balance of Power or the Correlation of Forces?

"...the ABM treaty and the offensive freeze,....were either a turning point or another impulse to the superpower arms race, either an augury of a more peaceful international order or a pause before a new set of crises."[1]
-Henry Kissinger

"The first summit allowed both sides to overcome strong mutual suspicions and become engaged in more constructive relationships, though they continued to pursue their own goals in the international arena."[2]
-Anatoly Dobrynin

In the 1970s the United States and the Soviet Union, the world's two superpowers, sought to control the growth of the world's deadliest weapons. During the preceding twenty-five years, both nations had built massive nuclear arsenals. The fear that the Cold War could turn nuclear overrode every other aspect of US-Soviet relations.

By reaching agreements leading to the Interim Agreement on Offensive Weapons and the Anti-ballistic Missile Treaty (collectively known as the first Strategic Arms Limitation Treaty or SALT I), Kissinger and Dobrynin successfully bridged their respective governments' competing visions of the superpower relationship as well as overcame Washington's and Moscow's differing goals for arms control. They also made substantial progress towards a second treaty culminating in the 1974 Vladivostok Accords. However, SALT II was not signed until after Kissinger left office. The telephone transcripts showed that Kissinger and Dobrynin were successful in reaching arms control agreements because each perceived that the other was well-intentioned and truly committed to preventing nuclear war.

Arms Control and Detente

After the Americans exploded atomic bombs over Hiroshima and Nagasaki to end the Second World War in 1945, from the mid-1950s to mid-1960s they developed intercontinental ballistic missiles (ICBMs) and

---

[1] Henry Kissinger, *White House Years* (New York: Simon & Schuster, 1979), 1244.

[2] Anatoly Dobrynin, *In Confidence – Moscow's Ambassador to America's Six Cold War Presidents* (New York: Times Books, 1995), 258.

intermediate-range ballistic missiles (IRBMs).[3] The Atlas and Titan I ICBMs had ranges of 5,000 miles, and were succeeded by the Minuteman and Titan II.[4] The US also produced the Thor and Jupiter IRBMs (stationed in Great Britain, Italy, and Turkey and therefore surrounding the Soviet Union), as well as the submarine-launched ballistic missile (SLBM) Polaris.[5]

In 1949 the Soviet Union detonated its first atomic weapon. By 1957 it had tested an ICBM, with mass production under way two years later.[6] In the summer of 1962 the Soviets began constructing sites in Cuba for the installation of intermediate range nuclear missiles capable of travelling 2,000 miles and hitting the Panama Canal as well as most American cities, leading to the Cuban Missile Crisis.[7] After the crisis passed, Moscow initiated an arms buildup under Leonid Brezhnev in 1964. For the next twenty years, Soviet defense spending increased by an average of 4-5 percent annually in real terms.[8]

By considering arms control, both Democratic and Republican administrations in the United States tacitly acknowledged that the Soviets had significantly narrowed the gap in strategic weapons. There would have been little reason for the United States to limit its nuclear arsenal and allow the Soviet Union to catch up if Washington still held a significant advantage. Consequently, the Johnson administration first proposed arms control in 1966, but Moscow did not commit until 1968 as they approached parity.[9] However, the Soviet invasion of Czechoslovakia that year delayed negotiations until the administration of Richard Nixon.[10] According to Lawrence Freedman, Professor of War Studies at London's King's College, by 1970 the Soviets had matched the Americans in

---

[3] James M. Morris, *America's Armed Forces – A History* (Englewood Cliffs, New Jersey: Prentice Hall, 1991), 324.

[4] Ibid.

[5] Ibid.

[6] Bevin Alexander, *How America Got It Right – The U.S. March To Military and Political Supremacy* (New York: Crown Forum, 2005), 167.

[7] Ibid., 170.

[8] Eric Hobsbawm, *The Age of Extremes – A History of the World, 1914-1991* (New York: Pantheon Books, 1994), 246.

[9] John Whiteclay Chambers II, ed. *The Oxford Companion to American Military History* (New York: Oxford University Press, 1999), s.v. "SALT Treaties," by Raymond L. Garthoff.

[10] Ibid.

ICBMs and also made great gains in SLBMs.[11] He added that the USSR maintained superiority in both throughout much of the decade, while the US retained a large edge in bombers and overall missile quality.[12] At the time of the first summit between Nixon and Brezhnev in May, 1972, the totals for each in ICBMs, SLBMs and bombers were: United States –1054, 656, and 450; Soviet Union –1607, 740, and 200.[13]

US-Soviet Strategic Weapons Totals at the time of SALT I (1972)

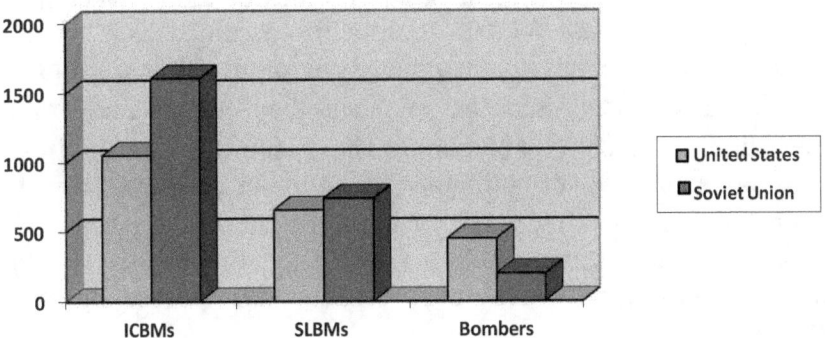

For the Americans arms control was a practical response to the reality that a balance of power existed between the United States and the Soviet Union. A rough equivalence in strategic weapons required a change in strategy for Washington. The US could no longer rely upon its overwhelming nuclear superiority to prevent a Soviet attack on itself or its allies in Western Europe. Nuclear parity ensured mutually assured destruction (MAD) – the certainty that if either nation attacked the other, retaliation and millions of dead on both sides would be the result. Nixon and Kissinger believed that despite no longer possessing a nuclear preponderance, they could maintain international stability by agreeing with Moscow to limit their respective nuclear arsenals.

Rather than a balance of power, for the Soviet Union arms control negotiations provided further evidence that the long-awaited and inevitable "correlation of forces" was occurring. According to Marxist-Leninist theory, these political and economic forces would propel

---

[11] Lawrence Freedman, *The Evolution of Nuclear Strategy*, 3rd ed. (New York: Palgrave Macmillan, 2003), 329.
[12] Ibid.
[13] Iwan W. Morgan, *Beyond the Liberal Consensus – A Political History of the United States Since 1965* (New York: St. Martin's Press, 1994), 71.

socialism to worldwide preeminence. The Soviets viewed the attainment of nuclear parity as an important step in this process. Thus while balance of power theory implied that the two superpowers had achieved a stabilization of international relations, the correlation of forces doctrine suggested a changing of the guard in world politics.

Balance of Power

Balance of power – a classic theory of international relations – grew out of the European great power politics of the nineteenth century. According to Kenneth Waltz, the theory assumed that states were individual actors in an international system of nations struggling for survival.[14] The states used the methods they had available for self-preservation or even domination.[15] These could be internal, such as increasing economic or military strength, or external by forming relationships with another nation or group of nations.[16] Balance of power also presumed that states would act rationally, that is they would never initiate a conflict in which they were certain to lose or even face annihilation.

A.F.K. Organski and Jacek Kugler explained that according to balance of power theory, when power was relatively balanced between states or groups of states there would be peace.[17] In contrast, when power became unevenly distributed, the chances of war increased.[18] In such a case the stronger nation or group of nations which always sought to maximize its power would attack the weaker.[19]

The balance of power and relative stability of post-World War II Europe was not the intentional creation of either of the superpowers in the view of John J. Mearsheimer. In fact, self-interested nations often created stability inadvertently through actions designed to ensure their security, but not necessarily peace.[20] The Americans supported Western Europe with economic and military resources to lessen the chances of a successful

---

[14] Kenneth N. Waltz, *Theory of International Politics* (New York: McGraw-Hill, Inc., 1979), 118.

[15] Ibid.

[16] Ibid.

[17] A.F.K. Organski and Jacek Kugler, "Causes, Beginnings and Predictions," in *The War Ledger* (Chicago: University of Chicago Press, 1980), 14.

[18] Ibid.

[19] Ibid., 15.

[20] John J. Mearsheimer, *The Tragedy of Great Power Politics* (New York: W.W. Norton & Company, 2001), 49.

Soviet attack which could alter the balance of power.[21] Likewise, the Soviets' claimed that their occupation of Eastern Europe was an effort to preserve their security.

Of course, the Cold War introduced a new component to balance of power politics: nuclear weapons. Despite the fact that the United States and the Soviet Union had reached a level of mutually assured destruction by the 1970s, this did not rule out the possibility of a conventional war as long as both sides believed such a conflict would not escalate into a nuclear one, according to Mearsheimer.[22] The answer is not certain because as he pointed out, "(thankfully) there is not much history to draw on."[23] Nevertheless, even in the age of MAD both nations continued to have security concerns and desired a balance in conventional as well as nuclear forces.[24]

The Correlation of Forces

Another theory of international relations, the Soviet doctrine of the correlation of forces, differed from balance of power theory in both its origins and policy implications. Julian Lider explained that Soviet scholars rejected balance of power because it was "traditional," "bourgeois," and an example of "political realism," a philosophy associated with the leading capitalist countries.[25] On the other hand, the idea of a correlation of forces derived from Marxist-Leninist theory that objective, scientifically provable laws governed the unfolding of history.[26] These laws dictated that socialism would eventually replace capitalism around the world, and the correlation of forces demonstrated these historical laws in action.[27] Finally, while Nixon and Kissinger applied balance of power theory to a world they saw as multi-polar due to the rise of China, Western Europe, and Japan, the Soviet correlation of forces concept implied two blocs of nations with irreconcilable differences.[28]

---

[21] Ibid.

[22] Ibid., 131.

[23] Ibid.

[24] Ibid., 132.

[25] Julian Lider, "The Correlation of World Forces: The Soviet Concept," *Journal of Peace Research* Vol. 17, No. 2, Special Issue on Imperialism and Militarization (1980), 163.

[26] Ibid., 151.

[27] Ibid.

[28] Ibid.

According to William B. Husband, Moscow believed that Washington's foreign policy was based purely on military strength, particularly as demonstrated by American reliance on "nuclear intimidation" to advance its interests at the end of World War II.[29] The Soviets believed this approach to international affairs was terribly misguided because it ignored or undervalued the importance of "political and economic processes as vital historical forces," wrote Husband.[30] These included the withering of the old European colonial empires, the spread of socialism to many newly independent nations in Africa, Asia, and Latin America, and the economic resurgence of capitalist nations like West Germany and Japan. From Moscow's perspective, Washington had only changed course and sought arms control after "international setbacks" resulting from these political and economic changes around the globe.[31]

The Soviets believed that capitalism faced a crisis around the globe "*as a system*," wrote Lider (italics in original).[32] With the ability to blunt the power of America's reactionary impulses, Soviet military parity would allow the laws of social development to unfold naturally. Thus the Marxist-Leninist doctrine of the inevitability of war between socialism and capitalism was "replaced by the assumption of the inevitability of the ideological struggle" between rival blocs of nations led by the United States and the Soviet Union, according to Lider.[33] Consequently, Husband explained that the Soviets were genuinely interested in arms limitations and lessening the dangers of nuclear war.[34] Indeed, they welcomed peace due to their certainty that in a long-term and non-military ideological struggle, the eventual triumph of socialism was preordained by the laws of history.[35]

Power Transition Theory

Rather than a balance of power or the correlation of forces, another theory of international relations may provide a better explanation for what

---

[29] William B. Husband, "Soviet Perceptions of U.S. 'Positions-of-Strength' Diplomacy in the 1970s," *World Politics* Vol. 31, No. 4 (Jul., 1979), 496.

[30] Ibid.

[31] Ibid., 496, 497.

[32] Lider, 156.

[33] Ibid.

[34] Husband, 505.

[35] Ibid., 505, 507.

was taking place in the US-Soviet strategic relationship during the 1960s and 1970s. Organski and Kugler rejected balance of power theory, espousing power transition theory instead. It originated in the 1950s and held assumptions directly at odds with the balance of power interpretation.[36] It argued that nations were *more* likely to go to war when they had similar political, economic, and military strength if one was seeking to surpass the other, and in case of war the initiator of conflict would come from the *weaker* side, not the one holding greater power.[37] This was because under power transition theory it was not the stronger nation, or the defender, which acted in order to maximize its strength and influence, but the weaker nation, called the challenger, which behaved aggressively due to its dissatisfaction with the international status quo.[38] The chances of war increased when the challenger reached a level of strength equal to eighty percent or higher of the dominant nation's GNP.[39] Therefore, unlike balance of power theory which stated that changes in alliances caused a redistribution of power, power transition theory assumed that changes in power resulted from developments within nations.[40] The Soviet military buildup in the years after the Cuban Missile Crisis of 1962 could be interpreted as an example of such an internal development.

Did the Soviet Union in the 1960s and 1970s meet the description of an unsatisfied challenger seeking to make a power transition and surpass the dominant nation – the United States? It seems plausible in light of a cursory overview of US-Soviet relations during the post-World War II period. Ronald L. Tammen explained how a cold war develops whenever a nation is dissatisfied with its status in the international arena, yet lacks the means to do anything about it.[41] During times such as these, there may be relative stability between states, but not without animosity.[42] The Soviet withdrawal behind the Iron Curtain at the start of the Cold War could be seen as an unsatisfied state refusing to participate in the US-

---

[36] Organski and Kugler, 19.

[37] Ibid., 19, 51.

[38] Ibid.

[39] Ibid., 49.

[40] Ibid., 24.

[41] Ronald L. Tammen, et al., *Power Transitions: Strategies for the 21st Century* (New York: Chatham House Publishers, 2000), 12.

[42] Ibid.

engineered post-war international order, suggested Tammen.[43] However, over the course of the next twenty-five years the Soviet Union grew into a potential challenger, mostly on the strength of nuclear weapons.[44] Although they had attained a rough nuclear parity, Tammen stipulated that the Soviets remained behind the Americans in overall power due to "deficiencies in political, economic, and social resources."[45]

Nevertheless, it is difficult to overlook the dramatic increase in Soviet military spending in the 1960s and 1970s. Douglas Lemke and Suzanne Werner defined a challenger to the status quo as dissatisfied "if the prospective rules of the system that it would like to impose are different 'enough' from those already established by the current dominant country."[46] Certainly the contrast between Soviet socialism and American capitalism seemed to meet this description. In addition, Lemke and Werner argued that an increase in military spending by the challenger relative to that spent by the dominant nation could signal a willingness to wage war.[47] However, if the dominant nation built up at a faster rate than the challenger, it could indicate that it was more dedicated to preserving the status quo than the challenger was to upsetting it.[48] Thus the US military buildup under Ronald Reagan during the 1980s could be viewed as an attempt to offset Soviet efforts at completing a power transition.

Lemke and Werner used two factors to determine if a nation was committed to changing the status quo. First, a country had to undergo an extraordinary military buildup, defined as "[w]henever the average annual military increase within a decade is greater than the cumulative annual average for all previous years."[49] Second, the nation's "extraordinary military expenditure increase for the decade in question minus the dominant country's military expenditure increase for the decade" had to exceed zero.[50] In other words, the challenger had to be building up faster than it had ever done previously, and at a greater rate than the dominant nation. By this standard, the Soviet Union was committed to change

---

[43] Ibid.

[44] Ibid., 47, 55.

[45] Ibid., 55.

[46] Douglas Lemke and Suzanne Werner, "Power Parity, Commitment to Change, and War," *International Studies Quarterly* Vol. 40, No. 2 (Jun., 1996), 239.

[47] Ibid., 240.

[48] Ibid.

[49] Ibid., 244.

[50] Ibid.

during the 1970s because its extraordinary military buildup was greater than US military expenditures.[51] However, it should be noted that using these metrics, the Soviet Union could be identified as committed to change throughout much of its existence, particularly during Stalin's forced rapid industrialization program in the 1930s.[52]

The differential in military expenditures was reflective of the Soviet buildup, but also of the American build-down as the US sought to disengage from the Vietnam War. In 1970, US defense spending represented 40.8% of the total federal budget.[53] By 1978 it had fallen to 23.8%, the lowest since the Second World War.[54] Although the USSR did not surpass the United States in total power by the end of the détente period, the difference narrowed, and according to Organski and Kugler it was "precisely, the relationship between the challenger and the dominant country that, in the transition model, [was] likely to occasion a major war."[55] Furthermore, "the model insist[ed] that attempts to arrest the gains of the faster-growing nation [would] fail."[56] The challenger's eventual completion of the power transition past the dominant nation was all but certain.[57]

Because it was the nuclear age, however, the Soviets and Americans never confronted each other directly. According to power transition theory, throughout the 1970s the US desired to remain the dominant power and sought to preserve the international status quo, while the USSR attempted to disrupt it in Asia, Africa, and Latin America.[58] The purpose behind destabilization was to effect "a more pro-Soviet alignment," and eventually "abet an open challenge to the United States at the global level," wrote Tammen.[59] Consequently, the US and the USSR found themselves on opposite sides of revolutionary national liberation movements around the world.

---

[51] Ibid., 250.

[52] Ibid., 249, 250.

[53] Morgan, 72.

[54] Ibid.

[55] Organski and Kugler, 25.

[56] Ibid., 28.

[57] Ibid.

[58] Tammen, 57.

[59] Ibid.

SALT I

SALT I represented an effort to preserve the US-Soviet strategic equilibrium. Signed by Nixon and Brezhnev on May 26, 1972, at the first Moscow summit, the treaty embodied a rough balance between each arsenal.[60] The Interim Offensive Agreement froze the number of each side's ICBMs and SLBMs for five years.[61] At the moment of signing, the Soviets outnumbered the Americans in total missile launchers (ICBMs and SLBMs) 2,348 to 1,710.[62] The addition of Soviet ICBMS under construction at the time eventually raised the total to 2,359.[63] However, the US had developed the technology to equip missiles with multiple independently-targeted re-entry vehicles (MIRVs) or multiple nuclear warheads on a single missile – something the Soviets had not yet even tested.[64] Additionally, SALT I did not apply to strategic bombers where the US held a significant advantage.[65]

Although the agreement only enacted temporary limits, Dobrynin explained that the five-year interim period was to allow time for further negotiations leading to actual reductions in the numbers of weapons.[66] Kissinger called the treaty, "a snapshot, as of the moment of signature, of the strategic relationship as it had evolved over the previous decade."[67] He claimed that the Soviets had dramatically increased ICBM construction after the Cuban Missile Crisis in 1962.[68] Indeed, while the American ICBM total had held at 1,054 since 1965, the Soviet force increased from 570 in 1967, to 900 in 1968, to 1050 in 1969.[69] Kissinger explained that by the time of the SALT signing, Moscow had long surpassed Washington in ICBMs.[70]

As limited as SALT I was, it is difficult to overstate the importance of at least initiating arm control negotiations due to the

---

[60] Richard Nixon, *RN – The Memoirs of Richard Nixon* (New York: Grosset & Dunlap, 1978), 616.
[61] Ibid.
[62] Chambers, ed., Garthoff.
[63] Freedman, 340.
[64] Henry Kissinger, *Years of Upheaval* (New York: Simon & Schuster, 1982), 256.
[65] Ibid., 257.
[66] Dobrynin, *In Confidence*, 257.
[67] Kissinger, *Years of Upheaval*, 256.
[68] Ibid.
[69] Adam Ulam, *Dangerous Relations – The Soviet Union in World Politics, 1970-1982* (New York: Oxford University Press, 1983), 47.
[70] Kissinger, *Years of Upheaval*, 256.

completely unprecedented and unimaginably destructive power of nuclear weapons. The US atom bomb dropped on Nagasaki at the end of World War II, "Fat Man," as well as the first Soviet atomic weapon detonated in 1949 each released about 20 kilotons or 20,000 tons of TNT.[71] In 1952 the US detonated the first thermonuclear weapon, which yielded 10,000 kilotons or 10,000,000 tons of TNT – the equivalent of *five-hundred* Nagasakis![72] In the years leading up to détente and throughout the end of the Cold War, both nations built more of these devastatingly powerful "megaton" bombs with the explosive power of a million or more tons of TNT.[73]

Structural differences in the American and Soviet nuclear arsenals greatly complicated arms control. Usually the best that negotiators could agree upon was a rough equivalence, and so both nations had to be willing to allow the other numerical superiority in some areas in order to achieve an approximate overall balance. For example, the Soviet Union based their force structure primarily on large, ground-launched ICBMs. Geographical proximity to Europe, the original Cold War battlefield, as well as a lack of ports dictated that Soviet reliance on air and submarine-launched weapons would be secondary. In contrast, the distance of the United States from Europe as well as America's dual coastlines necessitated a more diversified arsenal – the nuclear "triad": ground-based ICBMs, submarines, and perhaps most significantly to Moscow – bombers. US aircraft in Europe and on aircraft carriers in the surrounding waters deeply concerned the Soviets, but the Americans never wanted to include these forward-based systems in negotiations.[74] This probably reflected American concerns that if its allies in Western Europe went unprotected, the Soviets might take military action with their superior conventional forces (tanks and troops). Meanwhile, the Americans were worried about Soviet superiority in both the number of ICBMs and in total "throw weight" (total lifting power of missiles – this issue grew in importance as the practice of equipping missiles with multiple warheads became prevalent). Additionally, as talks dragged on both sides continued to conduct research and improve their arsenals, leading Dobrynin to

---

[71] Thomas C. Reed, *At the Abyss – An Insider's History of the Cold War* (New York: Ballantine Books, 2004), 22; Freedman, xiii.

[72] Ibid.,22.

[73] Freedman, xiii.

[74] Dobrynin, *In Confidence*, 216.

observe that "military technology was running ahead of the protracted negotiations."[75]

Differences between the American and Soviet government bureaucracies added to the complexity. Kissinger had far more knowledge about American military planning and weaponry than Dobrynin did of Soviet military matters. As a member of the National Security Council, Kissinger had access to the Secretary of Defense and the President. After adding the title of Secretary of State, Kissinger had his feet in both the military and diplomatic realms of the federal government. Ultimately, however, Kissinger answered exclusively to Nixon.

In contrast, Dobrynin had many bosses, but less access to information. Any message that he passed to Kissinger had to first be approved by the Politburo membership.[76] Furthermore, Dobrynin claimed that he and other members of the Foreign Ministry communicated only sparingly with the Defense Ministry. He gave the impression that he learned more about the Soviet arsenal from Americans like Kissinger than from his own military. In 1994 while at a conference attended by former Soviet and US officials entitled "SALT II and the Growth of Mistrust," Dobrynin explained: "Military planning in Russia was top secret. It's unbelievable: in your country, it's a loose cannon. You discuss all military things, rightly or wrongly."[77] He added that Moscow would give him instructions such as: "'Do not compromise on this issue; merely inform the Americans of our position on this issue.'"[78] Since diplomacy and defense were kept separate, Dobrynin asserted that he never really knew what his government's long term military plans were.[79] Perhaps most surprisingly, Dobrynin claimed that he and others in the Foreign Ministry did not even know the names of their weapons, so they used American names for Soviet weapons instead.[80] For example, when discussing the Soviet bomber called *Backfire* by the Americans,

---

[75] Ibid., 217.

[76] Vladislav Zubok, *A Failed Empire – The Soviet Union in the Cold War from Stalin to Gorbachev* (Chapel Hill: University of North Carolina Press, 2007), 216.

[77] The Carter-Brezhnev Project, "SALT II and the Growth of Mistrust," Thomas J. Watson Institute for International Studies (Brown University, 1994), 158. Available at http://www.gwu.edu/~nsarchiv/NSAEBB/NSAEBB313/doc14.pdf.

[78] Ibid.

[79] Ibid.

[80] Ibid., 159.

participants at the aforementioned conference erupted in laughter when Dobrynin asked: "By the way, why is it *Backfire* and not *Forwardfire*?"[81]

Under Nixon, American nuclear strategy diverged from that of his Cold War predecessors. Presidents Truman, Eisenhower, Kennedy, and Johnson had all maintained varying degrees of US nuclear superiority over the USSR.[82] However, at his first presidential press conference on January 27, 1969, Nixon declared that his administration would pursue "'sufficiency not superiority'" in nuclear weapons.[83] This strategy shaped Nixon's vision of arms control, which did not require both sides to have identical arsenals. First, Nixon viewed the Soviets as a land power and the U.S. as a sea power.[84] Second, he argued that while the Soviet Union had larger weapons, America had better weapons.[85] Third, even if it was possible politically and financially to counter the Soviet buildup and reach superiority in each and every category of weaponry, it would be long after both nations had already acquired the means to destroy each other.[86] Additionally, from the time of their first meeting with Dobrynin on February 17, 1969, Nixon and Kissinger made it clear that progress on arms control would have to be connected to Soviet cooperation in resolving various international problems including the Vietnam War and West German access to Berlin.[87] The policy became known as linkage.

The SALT negotiations took place on two levels: the official talks and through the backchannel. For almost three years the official negotiations alternated between Helsinki, Finland and Vienna, Austria, with Gerard Smith and Vladimir Semenov leading the American and Soviet delegations respectively.[88] The backchannel discussions between Kissinger and Dobrynin took over if the two sides reached an impasse.[89] As Kissinger explained, "[w]henever a deadlock persisted in these formal talks," he and Dobrynin "would work out an agreement in principle on the stalemated issue," leaving technical details as well as language to the

---

[81] Ibid.

[82] Jonathan Aitken, *Nixon – A Life* (Washington, D.C.: Regnery Publishing, Inc., 1993), 433.

[83] Ibid.

[84] Nixon, 415.

[85] Ibid.

[86] Ibid.

[87] Aitken, 434.

[88] Kissinger, *White House Years*, 1216.

[89] Ibid.

formal delegations.[90] Likewise, Dobrynin explained how the backchannel served as "a more convenient means for both governments to compromise a deadlock and reach a final decision at the crucial moments of negotiation."[91] Both lamented that members of the official negotiating teams did not receive enough credit for their work.

Establishing nuclear equivalence between arsenals with different force structures was perhaps the most significant obstacle in the earliest discussions. For example, in a conversation from July 28, 1970, Kissinger referenced the Soviet SS-9s, 300 extra-large ICBMs of which the United States had no equivalent:

> K: I am sitting on [the] back patio thinking about peaceful coexistence.

> D: Good for you, Henry. I am living with the same thought. I will be in Moscow thinking in the same way.

Then later:

> K: When are you leaving?

> D: Tomorrow night.

> K: When are you coming back?

> D: I hope by four weeks—just enough to gain strength to conduct discussions.

> K: That will give you an unfair advantage.

> D: What about you?

> K: I am working on the budget. You are building so many SS-9's. You are upsetting the balance.[92]

---

[90] Ibid.

[91] Dobrynin, *In Confidence*, 219.

[92] [February 1970-March 1971. Box #27.] *Henry A. Kissinger Telephone Conversation Transcripts (Telcons): [Anatoly Dobrynin File]*. Richard Nixon Presidential Library and Museum, Yorba Linda, California. National Archives and Records Administration.

Despite the playful tone, Kissinger had raised a potentially significant issue for the SALT negotiations. As he explained, the Nixon administration's predecessors had based American strategic forces on small, accurate missiles such as the Minuteman ICBM and the Poseidon SLBM, both of which were designed to carry MIRVs.[93] On the other hand, the Soviet arsenal featured less accurate, but larger missiles capable of carrying greater payloads, meaning that once the Soviets developed MIRVs, they could potentially deliver more of them in a single launch.[94] Kissinger believed that American technology could blunt the Soviet edge in size and strength of missiles, but not indefinitely.[95]

The backchannel did not always run smoothly at first. During arms control discussions the Soviets were chiefly interested in an anti-ballistic missile (ABM) treaty to limit American defensive weapons. The Soviets feared that an American ABM system could protect the United States from a missile attack, thereby mitigating the effect of Moscow's superior ICBM arsenal. Thus the Americans would be in a position to launch a possible first-strike while remaining confident that their ABM system would protect them from the ensuing Soviet retaliatory second strike. On the other hand, the Americans were concerned about the massive build-up of Soviet offensive nuclear weapons since the 1960s. Eventually, the White House made a proposal through the backchannel to link an antiballistic missile treaty with a second agreement to temporarily freeze offensive weapons. Before the Kremlin responded however, Soviet arms control negotiator Vladimir Semenov began discussing a strikingly similar proposal with his American counterpart in the regular diplomatic negotiations in Vienna, Ambassador Gerard Smith.[96] This led to the following conversation between Kissinger and Dobrynin on May 11, 1971:

> K: I just had a talk with Gerry Smith and apparently our channel in not working properly. Semonov [sic] is going along accepting my proposition to you which Gerry Smith doesn't know about…

---

[93] Kissinger, *White House Years*, 197, 212.

[94] Ibid., 197-198.

[95] Ibid., 198.

[96] Ibid., 817, 147.

D: Semenov didn't have instructions and I have a telegram that says it.

K: Semenov on a boat trip went into great detail and Smith is so surprised that he has propositions we didn't make to him. Proposed ABM agreement, a freeze on offensive missiles— Smith never heard of it…

D: He has no authority.

K: We are in the position now that as far as Smith is concerned a Soviet proposition exists and the President doesn't have a response to his proposal.

D: They haven't discussed it in the govt. I know what I am telling you. The [Foreign] Minister [Andrei Gromyko] directed him and he is not authorized. Gromyko is not deceiving me.

K: The President can only conclude one of two things. Either there's confusion in Moscow which we don't believe or a deliberate attempt to mobilize his people against him or by-pass him.

D: It's not so. On this matter Semonov has no authority. What [sic] he makes a hint—I don't know.

K: In order to keep our channel intact and avoid on either side a refusal…Now we are in a position that as far as I am concerned it has to be treated formally. [outside of the backchannel] Smith is telling everyone what Semenov said…[97]

If the White House had made a proposal through the backchannel and not received a response via the same route, this could present several problems. First of all, as Kissinger told Dobrynin, Nixon would take it "as a personal affront," adding "What would Brezhnev think if he proposed to

[97] [April 1971-August 1971. Box #27.]

us through a channel and we went to a subordinate official and made a reply,[?]"[98] Secondly, if diplomatic subordinates were in discussions on a proposal before there was an agreement at the top, it could create bureaucratic momentum resulting in one side or the other feeling pressured into making a decision they had not intended to, simply because they did not want to appear as being obstructionist. Needless to say, this was not an auspicious beginning to the relationship.

The conversation became heated as both men attempted to determine what had gone wrong:

K: We have a serious problem now—

D: ??? reply. [sic]

K: We have to construct a reply from Smith to Semonov and I can't say it's not the Soviet position because no one knows I have talked with you.

D: I know the story and you must way [say] what you will to the President. Semonov when I was in Moscow he was told not to talk.

K: I don't understand it. You can reject the proposal but why when we are trying to do so many things…

D: Only two days ago I_____that emphasized the same point. If you do not believe it—

K: There's no sense in your lying. I just want to be sure you want to work with me.

D: This case they discuss through you and me. [The Kremlin has] No reason for misleading me.

Then later:

---

[98] Ibid.

K: You can argue with me but the fact is our government believes you have made a formal proposition to which we have to reply and the President believes he made a proposition to you and you are replying in a bureaucratic channel and he will think you are trying to box him in. It's not going to be considered a friendly gesture.

D: What can I say when I tell you it was not an intention? What else can I tell you?[99]

Despite his anger, Kissinger eventually calmed down and was willing to give Dobrynin the benefit of the doubt. "I will grant that this was done in good faith on your side," he said.[100] Even at this early point in their relationship, Kissinger seems to have begun to trust Dobrynin – a little. Dobrynin then asked if Semenov's proposal to Smith had been official, adding "Semenov can discuss many things for 5 hours and you can construe what you want and he will say he said nothing. Was it formal?"[101] Kissinger replied that Semenov had made the same proposal that Deputy National Security Advisor Alexander Haig had given Dobrynin through the channel.[102] Dobrynin then assured Kissinger: "[Semenov] has his instructions. I don't know whether—I don't know. Semonov has to follow instructions or he will lose his job."[103]

After reviewing a memo from Smith and a telegram from Semenov, Kissinger and Dobrynin were able to reconstruct what had happened.[104] Apparently Semenov had put forward a previous Soviet proposal, already rejected by Kissinger, stating that any freeze of offensive weapons would only take place *after* an ABM deal had been reached. [105] The distinction was not insignificant. If an ABM treaty was signed first and subsequently the SALT talks broke down, it would leave the United States in the position of having agreed to limit its defensive weapons while leaving the Soviets with a substantial edge in offensive missiles and with no restrictions on continuing their buildup.

---

[99] Ibid.

[100] Ibid.

[101] Ibid.

[102] Ibid.

[103] Ibid.

[104] Ibid.

[105] Kissinger, *White House Years*, 817.

Having allowed the dust to settle, Kissinger and Dobrynin agreed to what would become the golden rule of their relationship: Nothing would ever be discussed with either "bureaucracy" until there was an agreement "in principle" in the backchannel.[106] "It's not in the good of our relationship that while you and I are discussing something, subordinates are discussing the same thing," said Kissinger.[107] "The crucial point is after 2 and a half years and months of discussions with you and me, we will get something important," he added.[108]

The Soviets eventually accepted the White House proposal. At the 1972 Moscow summit Nixon and Brezhnev signed SALT I, which included *both* a five-year interim agreement limiting the deployment of offensive nuclear weapons and an anti-ballistic missile treaty (ABM) permanently restricting defensive missiles. A misunderstanding that could have easily led to a breakdown in talks (as would later occur during the initial trip to Moscow by Secretary of State Cyrus Vance in 1977) instead resulted in one of the signal achievements of the détente era. It also served to remind both Dobrynin and Kissinger that during times of great stress and even frustration with each other that they could reach agreements and make progress in improving relations.

Critics of SALT I in the United States believed that by freezing the status quo, the treaty conceded numerical superiority to the Soviets and endangered US security. Kissinger's response to such charges amounted to: "if there was an imbalance, SALT did not create it; it reflected self-limiting decisions made over a decade."[109] Of course, this subtle attempt at criticizing previous administrations was just one of many instances where Kissinger portrayed himself as a kind of victim of political and historical circumstances. Nevertheless, he was hopeful that the mood of both the public and Congress would change during the Interim Agreement's five years and the United States could then begin "to catch up."[110] Furthermore, SALT I did not prevent either side from modernizing or improving their current stockpiles.[111] The US could proceed with research and development on new programs including the B-1 bomber, the MX missile, the cruise missile, and the Trident submarine-missile

---

[106] [April 1971-August 1971. Box #27.]

[107] Ibid.

[108] Ibid.

[109] Kissinger, *Years of Upheaval*, 257.

[110] Ibid.

[111] Ibid.

system.[112] As Kissinger put it, "We were determined to avoid ever again being in a situation where only the Soviets had strategic programs under way."[113]

SALT I faced criticism in the Soviet Union as well. According to Georgi Arbatov, a member of both the Soviet Academy of Sciences and the Central Committee of the Communist Party, Brezhnev "treated the military as a very important power base," and gave it "virtually anything it asked for."[114] However, arms control was an anathema to many in the Soviet military who viewed the weapons buildup with great pride. During one Politburo debate over SALT I, Defense Minister Marshall Andrei Grechko claimed that he was responsible for the nation's security and could not support the treaty.[115] Nevertheless, Brezhnev "insisted on approval of the text," wrote Arbatov.[116] Furthermore, the Soviet General Secretary argued that as commander-in-chief *he* was the rightful guardian of Soviet national security, and "ripped into Grechko," for implying anything to the contrary.[117]

Such interchanges help to illustrate an important point made by the former Director of the Central Intelligence Agency, Robert M. Gates. As an intelligence advisor for SALT, Gates observed that "internal negotiations in both our government and the Soviets' were probably tougher and dirtier than between the two countries."[118] Thus as supporters of detente and SALT, Dobrynin and Kissinger both faced domestic opposition to their diplomatic endeavors and undoubtedly could relate to each other's predicament.

After the signing in Moscow, there awaited another challenge for SALT I in the US Senate, where the *Constitution* required the treaty to be ratified by a two-thirds vote. Led by Senators Henry "Scoop" Jackson (D-Washington) and Barry Goldwater (R-Arizona), a coalition of conservatives expressed alarm at the rough equivalence formulation.[119]

---

[112] Kissinger, *White House Years*, 1246.

[113] Ibid., 1245.

[114] Georgi Arbatov, *The System – An Insider's Life in Soviet Politics* (New York: Random House, Inc., 1992), 201.

[115] Ibid.

[116] Ibid., 202.

[117] Ibid.

[118] Robert M. Gates, *From the Shadows – The Ultimate Insider's Story of Five Presidents and How They Won the Cold War* (New York: Simon & Schuster, 1996), 40, 46.

[119] Kissinger, *White House Years*, 1232.

According to Freedman, SALT I implied "a trade of Soviet numerical superiority in missiles for US superiority in technology and bombers."[120] However, Jackson and others sought an exact equivalence in total weapons or "'equal aggregates,'" something Kissinger believed was financially impossible at a time of defense cuts.[121] Jackson and his colleagues had to settle for an amendment to the treaty which required parity in future SALT treaties and specified that SALT I was in no way to be construed as allowing the United States to ever fall behind the Soviet Union in strategic security.[122]

The notion of amending a treaty after it had already been negotiated and signed must have been extremely concerning to the Soviets. On August 7, 1972, Kissinger spoke with Dobrynin and attempted to assuage Moscow's fears that Jackson's amendment would substantively alter the SALT I agreement:

> K: Now, Anatol, I wanted to talk to you about the Jackson Amendment.
>
> D: Yes.
>
> K: Here is what we have decided to do. We've been working with him [Jackson] all weekend.
>
> D: Yes.
>
> K: And it has now become a matter of prestige and so forth. So what we have done is to try to get his agreement to a formulation which is essentially meaningless.

Then later:

> K: ...What we are saying [in a White House statement] - - the Jackson amendment does not constitute a reservation or interpretation to the agreement in any legal sense.
>
> D: Yeah. Will it be statement by the White House, yes?

---

[120] Freedman, 340.

[121] Kissinger, *Years of Upheaval*, 1011.

[122] Ibid.

K: After it is transmitted, yes.

D: Yeah, it will be statement by the White House.

K: Yes.

D: Okay.

K: But we have also gotten him to change the amendment that you have seen. It has been totally emasculated now.

D: I would like to see if possible the text really.

K: Well, you will get it. I am sending it over to you.

D: Okay.[123]

This exchange implied that Kissinger either thought he had manipulated Jackson into watering down the language of the amendment, or that Jackson was not entirely sincere and merely wanted to sound hawkish on national security. However, it was Jackson's own assistant, Richard Perle, who wrote the amendment and later worked tirelessly in consultation with twenty-five senators to get it passed.[124]

After reviewing the proposed amendment, Dobrynin remained confused. He and Kissinger spoke again about an hour and a half later to clarify the situation:

K: Did you get that material?

D: Yes, I'm just reading it. You see, one question I would like to ask you really here. It was there before and it is now again in this one…you should request the President to seek a future treat[y] and that inter alia would not limit the United States to levels of intercontinental strategic forces

---

[123] [July 1972-September 1972. Box #27.]

[124] Jay Winik, *On the Brink – The Dramatic, Behind-the-Scenes Saga of the Reagan Era and the Men and Women Who Won the Cold War* (New York: Simon & Schuster, 1996), 56.

inferior to the [levels] provided for the Soviet Union. What do you really mean exactly because - -

Then later…

> K: Well, it doesn't mean one for one in each category. It means, you know, that the total strategic impact of these categories - - all of this is drawn from things which we've already publicly said.

> D: No, no; I know. This is rather a matter of interpretation for my own and for Moscow. It doesn't really mean one for one.

> K: It means the principle of equal security.

> D: The principle of equal security; not really one by one because - -

> K: Not one by one in each category.

> D: Oh, I see. So it doesn't really change what we signed upon?

> K: No.[125]

As they wrapped up the conversation, Dobrynin thanked Kissinger for his explanation and said that he thought the White House statement and the amendment would be acceptable to Moscow.[126] "Of course, you understand, Henry, that we have discussed with you on very informal basis," said Dobrynin.[127] Kissinger understood that Dobrynin could not unilaterally give his approval and that their conversation had just been "in a spirit of what we can do to help relations."[128] Kissinger added, "See how easy I am to get along with."[129] Dobrynin laughed as he thanked him

---

[125] [July 1972-September 1972. Box #27.]
[126] Ibid.
[127] Ibid.

[128] Ibid.
[129] Ibid.

again and said goodbye.[130] They had successfully maneuvered around a potential minefield. Arms control – one of the foremost goals of détente – had nearly been derailed by American domestic politics.

Another ratification-related conversation on September 18, 1972, was simultaneously revealing and potentially embarrassing. First, Dobrynin inquired as to how things were proceeding in the Senate:

> D: First, maybe you will tell me about SALT - - Not SALT, but about ratification.

> K: Yeah, I'll have a definite answer by tomorrow evening.

> D: Oh, I see.

> K: But I think we can manage it by the end of the week but I'll give you a definite date tomorrow.

> D: *Because this is really for our ratification.* [italics mine]

> K: Yeah, I understand that.[131]

It is apparent from this exchange that for Dobrynin and Kissinger much more than the SALT agreement was at stake. They had both spent a great deal of time and energy as well as faced a substantial amount of skepticism about détente back home, particularly so in Kissinger's case. Both viewed ratification as validating them and their diplomacy. Such a mutual investment in relaxing tensions was essential for détente's success. Kissinger then continued:

> K: I'm calling you about something else which is slightly embarrassing to me in the light of my discussions in Moscow.

> D: What about?

---

[130] Ibid.
[131] Ibid.

K: It's the following - - whenever they pass something through the Congress, our Congressional liaison people just type up a note for the President and get him to make a phone call to the sponsor saying, you know, he's glad it passed and I found out to my horror that the people did that with the Jackson Amendment and so he called Jackson today.

D: Uh-ooh!

K: And I, you know, hope it won't come out but if it does come out, I want you to know how it happened.

D: Yeah.

And later:

K: Well, I want to express my apologies.

D: Yeah, I understand

K: And it is no indication - - it is so stupid that I don't know how to express it but it may not come out publicly but I wanted you to hear it from me.

D: Yeah, I understand. It is better not to come but if it comes, what could you do? Nothing really.[132]

Kissinger understood that the *Jackson Amendment* had been a tough pill for the Soviet leadership to swallow. The White House reluctantly acquiesced in the amendment's attachment to the SALT I treaty in order to garner enough votes in the Senate for ratification. Still, the Soviets had been forced to sit by while it must have seemed like the Americans were changing the deal reached in Moscow merely three months before. If the White House appeared to be celebrating by congratulating Jackson on passing his amendment it could have seemed underhanded and two-faced to the Kremlin. Kissinger's apology as well as Dobrynin's understanding

---

[132] Ibid.

of this standard political procedure further indicated the developing empathy in their relationship.

ABM

Along with the Interim Agreement on offensive weapons, SALT I also included the Anti-Ballistic Missile Treaty (ABM). The United States and the Soviet Union each agreed that any missile defense system would not exceed a maximum of 200 launchers.[133] According to Raymond Garthoff, by limiting themselves to this "strategically insignificant" level of anti-ballistic missiles the superpowers "contributed to containing one important area of arms competition."[134]

Instead of deploying extensive anti-ballistic missile systems to defend themselves from a nuclear attack, the superpowers relied on mutually assured destruction (MAD) in order to deter one another. Richard K. Betts defined deterrence as "a strategy for combining two competing goals: countering an enemy and avoiding war."[135] It grew naturally from balance of power theory.[136] Prior to MAD, there had been various other theories of deterrence, particularly those of the Rand Corporation's Bernard Brodie. However, MAD was probably first associated with President Kennedy's Secretary of Defense Robert McNamara, and contended that a nation only needed enough nuclear weapons to deter an attack.[137] Nuclear stability would prevail as long as each side had the means to deter a first-strike by possessing enough weapons to destroy the other with a retaliatory second-strike.[138] The deployment of an extensive ABM system by either side would have threatened the delicate nuclear balance between the superpowers by

---

[133] Freedman, 338.

[134] Raymond L. Garthoff, *Détente and Confrontation: American-Soviet Relations from Nixon to Reagan* (Washington, D.C.: Brookings Institution, 1985), 188, 189.

[135] Richard K. Betts, "The Lost Logic of Deterrence," *Foreign Affairs* Vol. 92, No. 2 (March/April 2013): 88.

[136] Frank C. Zagare, "Reconciling Rationality with Deterrence: A Re-Examination of the Logical Foundations of Deterrence Theory," *Journal of Theoretical Politics* Vol. 16, No. 2 (2004): 107.

[137] Richard Holmes, ed. *The Oxford Companion to Military History* (Oxford: Oxford University Press, 2001), s.v. "Strategic Arms Limitation/Strategic Arms Reduction Talks," by Sebastian Roberts.

[138] Richard C. Thornton, *The Nixon-Kissinger Years – The Reshaping of American Foreign Policy*, 2nd ed. (St. Paul, Minnesota: Paragon House, 2001), xvii.

insulating a potential aggressor from retaliation, thereby making the risks of launching a first-strike less costly.[139]

From the beginning of the Nixon administration, Kissinger believed that one of the most attractive features of developing an anti-ballistic missile system would be the ability to offer to limit it in exchange for an offensive arms agreement.[140] Nixon agreed, stating "I felt that tactically we needed the ABM as a bargaining chip" because the Soviets already possessed such a system around Moscow.[141] Nixon reasoned that if the US entered SALT discussions without one, something else more valuable might have to be given up: "we had to have it in order to be able to agree to forgo it."[142] However, the development of an anti-ballistic missile system sparked great controversy in Washington. Some feared that it would be destabilizing and inaugurate a brand new arms race. When the Senate approved funding on August 6, 1969, it did so by the single tie-breaking vote of Vice-President Spiro Agnew.[143]

The linking of the ABM agreement to an offensive freeze proved to be a watershed moment for détente. It not only culminated in SALT I – arguably the greatest achievement in US-Soviet diplomacy up to that time – but also broke the Cold War ice after twenty-five years. In this conversation from March 26, 1971, Kissinger and Dobrynin brought up several remaining issues including how many ABM sites each side would be permitted to have, where they would be located, and when to initiate negotiations for the offensive freeze:

> K: You and I are going steady. We should exchange telephone numbers.

> D: That is right. I will give you my Moscow number. 290-2520.

> K: I will not ask you what the area code is.

> D: It is in Moscow.

---

[139] Holmes, ed., Roberts.

[140] Kissinger, *White House Years*, 208.

[141] Nixon, 415.

[142] Ibid.

[143] Steven F. Hayward, *The Age of Reagan – The Fall of the Old Liberal Order, 1964-1980* (Roseville, CA: Prima Publishing, 2001), 274.

K: I have talked to the President about it [your proposal] and do not completely understand it. Is this in response to our letter?

D: You do not? It is in connection with our last talk and your draft.

K: I will tell you how we are prepared to work it. We are prepared to agree in principle to separate ABM agreement. Then negotiators would begin discussion of what it would be like – [M]oscow versus Washington, Washington versus –

D: Only involved the place? How many etc?

K: At that point they would begin discussing what sort of agreement. Then when they know what sort of agreement would discuss radars and so forth. Simultaneously would discuss freeze. If that is possible agreement would be immediate.

D: I have to check but –

K: When they begin drafting agreement they should talk about freeze.

D: They would discuss how many, etc. I don't know. It seems to be a little bit in the later stage. The will argue about (how many radars and all the little things.)

K: Not crucial to us. After you say agreement on ABM – agreement has been reached.

D: What is your position?

K: Certain start on ABM but also discuss freeze.

D: Simultaneously concluded on separate agreement and freezing at the same time.

K: Exactly.[144]

Differences in the American and Soviet force structures complicated ABM negotiations just as they had the rest of the SALT talks. Consequently, just a week before the official May 20, 1971, announcement that the superpowers had reached an agreement on an offensive freeze and an ABM deal, Kissinger and Dobrynin still had a few details to work out. Dobrynin pushed for including the phrase "equal limitations" in the announcement while Kissinger objected, arguing that it made more sense to use "equitable limitations" since each side had different radars and weapons. Dobrynin was extremely anxious about agreeing to any wording which could potentially upset Moscow. As he explained, the terminology that the Politburo had decided upon was the result of numerous meetings involving the entire Soviet bureaucracy:

K: What do you want?

D: I would like to put it in terms of limitation of this agreement should be equal.

K: We aimed at drawing up the text of an agreement limiting ABMs; that such an agreement should be equitable.

D: It's not a question of both sides on an equal basis.

K: What do you mean by "equal." [?]

D: When I mentioned this to you...

K: What you propose is your problem.

D: I understand. Terms of limitation should be equal...

K: Except "equal" doesn't have any precise meaning in these terms.

---

[144] [February 1970-March 1971. Box #27.]

D: What you pur, "…terms of limitation will be the same."
I think "equal" but maybe "the same" or some other word.
I am only trying to be close to what we said, whether terms
should be "the same" or "close" or maybe something else.

K: The trouble with "equal" is that since our weapons and
radars are so different I am not in position to say this has to
be the same numbers. There has to be some flexibility.
"equitable" seems to me to be a good word.

Then later…

D: I hope some day [sic] you will be an ambassador and be
sitting in a capital not so close to your source of power.

K: I understand.

D: If it was my proposal… But they [the Kremlin] gave me
the text. To prepare a letter is one thing, but in drafting this
letter there were six meetings of the whole government.

K: You haven't changed the text. I think "equitable"
means much more than "just". Will you accept "should be
based on the principle of equality?"

D: On equality? All right.

K: On the principle of equality.

D: Can't you say it without "principle?"

K: It just doesn't make any sense.

D: "Principle of equality"….. "principle of equality". All
right. You are taking advantage of me. It's your native
language.

K: [sarcastically] You see, I want to tell you as a friend,
what we want to propose is an arrangement so that we can

keep 20 radars and you can keep one – we have to keep some flexibility for that. Now, I have had another long session with the President...are we through; have you any other complaints?

D: No.

K: You were easier to deal with when we bought Alaska.

D: We didn't have Kissinger then.[145]

Kissinger's witty reference to the US purchase of Alaska from Russia in 1867 as well as Dobrynin's pithy response showed that even when conversations became heated and they grew frustrated with one another, both remained capable of a little good-natured kidding.

ABM did not completely prohibit defensive weapons – each side was permitted to defend a few sites. The Soviets particularly wanted to defend Moscow, while the Americans focused more on their ICBM fields.[146] During a preliminary meeting in Moscow, Brezhnev proposed to Kissinger that each side protect its capital and one field.[147] On May 17, 1972, just days before the first summit, Kissinger told Dobrynin that Nixon had agreed to Brezhnev's idea.[148] Nevertheless, Dobrynin still hoped to cajole Kissinger into dropping the number of sites down to just one:

> D: Yes, I understand. But one ABM [is] just as good as
> two.
>
> K: Just stick with the formula which we discussed in
> Moscow.
>
> D: Moscow, yeah. Okay.
>
> K: Good.

---

[145] [April 1971-August 1971. Box #27.]
[146] [May 1972-June 1972. Box #27.]
[147] Ibid.
[148] Ibid.

D: Thank you.

K: In other words, we insist on accepting your proposals; that's a tough position for you to be in.

D: (laughter)[149]

When the ABM treaty finally achieved ratification, it allowed both nations to deploy just two sites – one for each country's capital and a second for an ICBM field.[150] Each site could have a maximum of one hundred land-based, stationary anti-ballistic missile launchers.[151] Dobrynin later called this "a grave mistake on both sides," and suggested that if the superpowers had agreed on a "zero option," the entire Strategic Defense Initiative (SDI) or "Star Wars" controversy of the 1980s could have been avoided.[152]

In 1974 by mutual agreement both the United States and the Soviet Union reduced the number of ABM sites to one, with the Soviets maintaining their system around Moscow and the Americans planning to protect a single missile field in Grand Forks, North Dakota.[153] Theoretically, having only one ABM location each strengthened deterrence even further. However, in 1975 and perhaps indicative of the general Congressional view of defense spending at the time, the US unilaterally cancelled plans for any ABM sites at all.[154] The remaining Soviet site at Moscow may have been more intended for protection against China than anyone else.[155] Furthermore, the ongoing development of MIRV technology threatened to make a realistic anti-ballistic missile defense system less likely anyway.[156]

Kissinger did not view the demise of an American ABM system as a total loss. For him ABM's prime purpose had been to motivate the Soviets to agree to a freeze in offensive strategic forces, which they did.[157]

---

[149] Ibid.

[150] William Tompson, *The Soviet Union under Brezhnev* (London: Pearson Education Limited, 2003), 48.

[151] Ibid.

[152] Dobrynin, *In Confidence*, 219.

[153] Kissinger, *White House Years*, 210; *Years of Upheaval*, 1166.

[154] Kissinger, *White House Years*, 210.

[155] Freedman, 338.

[156] Ulam, 77.

[157] Kissinger, *White House Years*, 210.

Nevertheless, he expressed regret at the Congressional decision to do away with an anti-ballistic missile defense system and claimed that he had only reluctantly agreed to it at the time.[158]

The ABM treaty became an issue once again in the 1980s during the Reagan administration. In 1983 satellite photographs identified a radar station at Krasnoyarsk in Siberia.[159] The construction of a second anti-ballistic missile site violated the ABM agreement as it had been revised by Nixon and Brezhnev in 1974 at the third summit. After years of denials, Soviet Foreign Minister Eduard Shevardnadze admitted in 1989 that "'the construction of this station, equal in size to the Egyptian pyramids, constituted an open violation of the ABM treaty.'"[160]

One of the original provisions of the ABM treaty stipulated that either party could withdraw from the agreement after providing six months' notice.[161] Thus, when President George W. Bush announced his intention to resume research on President Reagan's Strategic Defense Initiative, the US pulled out of the ABM agreement in 2002.

SALT II

The Vietnam experience as well as Watergate cast a pall over the SALT II negotiations. Although the Vietnam War was ending for the United States as Nixon's second term began in 1973, that conflict had already done significant damage to American self-confidence. While the US continued to engage in strategic arms limitations talks, Kissinger hoped to compensate for this by simultaneously increasing America's conventional forces. He portrayed himself as stuck between Congressional liberals resisting defense spending and conservatives opposing arms control due to its "ideological ambiguity."[162] Kissinger seemed to view the left as wanting to surrender to communism while the right wanted an anti-communist crusade. The combination of the struggle with Congress as well as the Watergate scandal led him to conclude that by the beginning of the President's second term, "the political and moral

---

[158] Ibid.

[159] Arnold Beichman, *The Long Pretense - Soviet Treaty Diplomacy From Lenin to Gorbachev* (New Brunswick, New Jersey: Transaction Publishers, 1991), 56.

[160] Ibid.

[161] Ulam, 77.

[162] Kissinger, *Years of Upheaval*, 260.

authority he [Nixon] needed to pursue simultaneously the military balance and a sophisticated policy of arms control was beginning to erode."[163]

Nevertheless, the talks continued. In the backchannel Kissinger began kidding Dobrynin about the possibility of completely eliminating the SS-9s, the Soviets' largest missiles. This served as a running joke between the two, with Dobrynin usually humoring his counterpart and then politely moving on to another subject. For example, on March 6, 1973, as part of the early discussions for SALT II, Dobrynin told Kissinger that Brezhnev had invited him to Moscow:

> K: When does he want me to come? I hope not before the second half of April.
>
> D: When will you be ready to come?
>
> K: Well, that depends on you. You're agreeing to all our propositions?
>
> D: Well, this is the point we're going to discuss with you. (laughter)
>
> K: Well, what would make a good impression, Anatol, - - I don't want to suggest to you but I think it would speed the SALT discussions if you proposed that you will dismantle all SS-9s in the next phase of SALT, we would make very rapid progress.
>
> D: Yeah.
>
> K: Just the big ones as a sign of good will.
>
> D: Yeah.
>
> K: (laughter)
>
> D: (laughter) I think it's a good idea.[164]

---

[163] Ibid.
[164] [March 1973. Box #27.]

Of course the 300 powerful Soviet SS-9s represented one of the principle areas of imbalance between the superpower arsenals, and undoubtedly drew the ire of Nixon's and Kissinger's conservative critics who demanded "perfect symmetry."[165] However, Kissinger remained unworried about an exact numerical equivalence in every weapons category, preferring to concern himself with overall strategic security.

By this time Kissinger and Dobrynin had been working together for well over four years. A conversation on May 26, 1973, while planning for the second summit demonstrated awareness on the part of both that they had started to build a shared history:

> HK: Do you know today is the anniversary of our agreeing to the SALT Agreement?
>
> AD: Yes, I know. You are an exception because usually Americans do not remember for a long time in their foreign policy, but you do.
>
> HK: Now Anatol...
>
> AD: (laughing)[166]

The discussion and the ability to poke fun at one another demonstrated a growing level of comfort and familiarity between two tough and experienced diplomats. They knew that they had accomplished a great deal and were optimistic about their chances for further success with SALT II and beyond.

The emerging capability to place multiple nuclear warheads upon a single missile presented one of the foremost challenges in the SALT II talks. These MIRVs (multiple independently-targeted re-entry vehicles) gave each side the potential to magnify its arsenal without violating SALT I's limits on missile construction. One missile could be used to launch multiple warheads, each of which could then hit a separate target. In this context, the presence of 300 heavy Soviet SS-9s with greater throw weight and hence an ability to carry more warheads than anything the Americans possessed was no joking matter. However, Nixon believed that one of the

---

[165] Kissinger, *Years of Upheaval*, 264.
[166] [May 1973-June 1973. Box #28.]

reasons the second summit in June, 1973, did not produce a SALT II agreement was that the Soviets were not far enough along in their MIRV program to be comfortable talking about limits.[167] A conversation from July 11, 1973, between Kissinger and Dobrynin illustrated this point. First, Kissinger expressed frustration that the Soviets had not responded to an American MIRV proposal:

> K: What we would like are some observations from you on the MIRV question. Not that you agree with us, but something that enables us to get a discussion started.
>
> D: Well you see on MIRV question, really, it looks to me my reaction, and this is not official reaction, but I think this one for us it looks to us just one to stop our development.
>
> K: Well, that...
>
> D: One sided and...
>
> K: No, no, but another possibility is that you destroy 60 SS-9s the first year and then we go from there. We take that very seriously.
>
> D: Well, Henry, let's put it...
>
> K: ...the trouble is we've made a proposal to you. You think it's one-sided. I understand that, because it is one-sided. So then, could you – I'm not even asking for a counterproposal, I'm just asking for something that enables me to react to it.[168]

To illustrate his point, Kissinger referenced their shared history. He reminded Dobrynin of how their previous negotiations on SALT I had evolved: "You see in '71 you said you must have only defense [referring to ABM] and then we said no it has to include offense [the Interim Agreement]."[169] Kissinger correctly recalled that although he and

---

[167] Nixon, 879.

[168] [July 1973-September 1973. Box #28.]

[169] Ibid.

Dobrynin were originally far apart on SALT I, they had at least put forward their initial positions when negotiations began. However, in the current case Kissinger argued "we're in no position to make a compromise because we don't really know what you have in mind."[170] Dobrynin stated that he understood, but needed to refer to Moscow, particularly in the case of something as technically complex as MIRVs.[171] The appeal to their past negotiations apparently worked, because a few days later on July 17 Dobrynin got back to Kissinger with news that the Soviets were indeed ready to begin discussing MIRV limits.[172]

Nixon appointed Kissinger to be his Secretary of State in 1973 as well as continue on as National Security Advisor. According to Dobrynin, Kissinger called him from San Clemente, California (location of Nixon's "western White House") on August 22, and informed him of the appointment.[173] Kissinger assured Dobrynin that things would continue as before, "including lunches and dinners," after he replaced outgoing Secretary William Rogers:

> D: Well [Will] I send you congratulations in a letter or how. You prefer now to be much more formal so to speak.
>
> K: And I won't insist on protocol, Anatol, if you just call me Excellency we'll get along fine.
>
> D: That is exactly what I will say. So congratulations, the very best. It is final I guess.
>
> K: Yeh, that's right, but of course I don't need to tell you that if anything it may make it easier to do the things you and I have been doing together.
>
> D: I think it will.[174]

Dobrynin opined that the change improved Soviet-American relations because it ended what he called "the confused and uncertain situation in

---

[170] Ibid.

[171] Ibid.

[172] Dobrynin, *In Confidence*, 290.

[173] Ibid., 277.

[174] [July 1973-September 1973. Box #28.]

which the White House kept the secretary of state and indeed his entire department in the dark."[175] Now it would be much easier to get agreements from the backchannel into the official negotiations and avoid the kind of problem which had occurred previously between Smith and Semenov.[176] The installment of Kissinger as Secretary of State in addition to maintaining his duties as National Security Advisor also indicated that Nixon was further tightening his grip on foreign policy.

1973 was also a significant year for the Soviet military. According to Kissinger, at that time the Soviets had four new missiles in development, two of which were MIRV-capable and in the testing stage by the summer.[177] The SS-17, a newer and lighter ICBM designed to replace the SS-11, could carry three or four warheads while the SS-18, a potential replacement for the huge SS-9, was capable of delivering eight warheads.[178] The Soviets considered these modernizations of earlier missiles and technically not violations of SALT I's limits.[179] However some critics alleged that the Soviet Union was getting around the treaty's ceilings on missiles by simply adding more warheads.[180] Although obviously a defender of the treaty, even Kissinger charged the Soviets with "using the quantitative freeze to engage in a qualitative race."[181] He feared a potential Soviet strike on the US Minuteman land-based ICBM forces by the middle of the eighties.[182]

Brezhnev's staunch support for arms control and détente was not enough to derail the Soviet military's agenda. Especially in the late 70s and early 80s "they got away with a lot," according to Arbatov.[183] Even after attaining parity in conventional and nuclear weapons, the military was able to "develop and accumulate arms of all types," he added.[184] Arbatov claimed that Moscow outpaced Washington in long-range strategic delivery systems, mega-tonnage, and throw weight, as well as in medium-range weapons.[185] Gates believed that the buildup "enabled the

---

[175] Dobrynin, *In Confidence*, 277.
[176] Ibid.
[177] Kissinger, *Years of Upheaval*, 1101.
[178] Ibid.
[179] Ibid.
[180] Hayward, 590.
[181] Kissinger, *Years of Upheaval*, 1101.
[182] Ibid.
[183] Arbatov, 202.
[184] Ibid., 203.
[185] Ibid.

Soviets to close the strategic gap and establish a favorable military balance in Europe, and offered them the potential to gain superiority in a number of areas – depending on what the United States did."[186] Although some asserted after the Cold War that Moscow's nuclear and conventional arsenal had not posed a serious threat, "few in either political party or in the American government generally in 1976 or 1977...would have agreed," wrote Gates.[187] Furthermore, he considered the "sober assessments of Soviet military power" by both the Ford and Carter administrations to be "quite accurate."[188]

The MIRV differential favoring the Americans as well as the Soviet potential to narrow the gap and ultimately overtake the US drove both sides to seek limitations. The Soviets also hoped to avoid the embarrassment of signing an agreement highlighting the fact that they had yet to actually deploy any MIRVed missiles. Cognizant of this fact, on June 5, 1974, Kissinger presented the following proposal:

> K: One other thing that I thought about on the SALT discussion we had yesterday. We have no interest in making you sign something that's embarrassing for you. I'm trying to figure out some way of expressing this in a way that the differential in numbers...If we expressed it for example in terms of each side will stop deployment as of a certain date or deploy up to "X" percent of its total force. You see what I mean? Whichever number is higher.

> D: To total existence.

> K: Supposing we said, each side will stop deployment of MIRV missiles as of and let's say March 1, 1975, let me just think out loud. That would stop our program at 1100. Or deploy up to "X" percent of its total force in MIRV missiles, whichever number is higher.

> D: "X" percent on what date?

---

[186] Gates, 109.

[187] Ibid.

[188] Ibid.

K: Well, through 1979. You see if we said whatever number you and we agree on, supposing it's 750, we could express that as a percentage of your total force.

D: Of total force, you mean on missiles?

K: Yes. You see in that way there wouldn't be any - - the agreement wouldn't look as if any differential were put in. If each side has the right to do the same thing.

D: I understand.

K: No, you won't have [to]

D: Mention to you about what we have now.

K: No, but you have the choice either to stop on March 1975 or to build up to 30 or 40 percent or whatever the number is we agree on, of your total force. Whichever number is higher. We would stop in March 1975. Or whenever we have 1100. You would go up to the percentage because in March '75 you won't have anything yet.

D: This is exactly the point.

K: I want to find a formula which sounds equivalent.[189]

According to Kissinger's plan, after a certain date the US would cease affixing MIRVs to its missiles. However, recognizing that the Soviets had yet to deploy any such weapons, Moscow would be permitted to do so until a predetermined percentage of their force had MIRVs. Kissinger was seeking to find a formula that limited both sides while avoiding mentioning any hard numbers. Dobrynin could then tell his superiors back in Moscow that they would not have to sign a treaty expressing a numerical differential: "We can state it in such a way that even if a

---

[189] [January 1974-August 1974. Box #28.]

differential results it will not be expressed in such an embarrassing manner," said Kissinger.[190]

Kissinger's offer would allow Dobrynin to save face with Moscow, and the USSR to save face with the US. It demonstrated Kissinger's desire to reach an accord, his respect for Dobrynin, and an understanding of the Soviets' need to be treated as a co-equal superpower. It epitomized the empathetic form of diplomacy necessary to bring about a thaw in Cold War tensions.

Later that month and amidst a Congressional investigation of Watergate, Nixon returned to Moscow for the third summit. The fact that the Soviets had yet to deploy any MIRVed missiles continued to complicate arms talks. This meant that any arrangement would probably result in only the US halting its MIRV program with the Soviets then being permitted to proceed until they had reached the agreed upon limit.[191] Such a deal would face strong opposition from conservatives in Congress. Consequently, Kissinger sought a freeze, but at a level which would give the United States a significant edge in MIRVs due to the Soviet overall superiority in ICBMs.[192] He reasoned that if the Soviets had more missiles, the US ought to be able to compensate by having more warheads. According to Nixon, Brezhnev did not see it that way and hence no SALT II agreement emerged from the third summit.[193]

Richard Nixon's resignation on August 9, 1974, in light of the Watergate affair posed several potential challenges for the Kissinger-Dobrynin relationship. Would the new president, Gerald Ford, adopt the policies of his predecessor? Would he be content to conduct relations with the Soviet Union through the backchannel? Dobrynin reported that when he had met with Ford at the Soviet embassy the previous January, the then Vice-President said that if he became president "'by the chance of fate'" he would continue détente and with Kissinger as his secretary of state.[194] Accordingly, the day before taking office Ford telephoned Kissinger and asked him to continue in his post at the State Department.[195] On August 12 Kissinger put Dobrynin at ease about the change of administrations, but

---

[190] Ibid.

[191] Nixon, 1031.

[192] Ibid., 1031-1032.

[193] Ibid., 1032.

[194] Dobrynin, *In Confidence*, 310.

[195] Henry Kissinger, *Years of Renewal* (New York: Simon & Schuster, 1999), 23.

not before kidding him about the nomination of an old nemesis to head the Defense Department:

> K: I was just talking to the President and he said: When is Dobrynin coming back? I said he's supposed to come back early in September but if I'm any judge of him, he'll be back long before that.

> D: (Laughter)

> K: I just got through saying it. You're making me a great man.

> D: (Laughter) Well, Brezhnev thought I would feel much better close to you than to being on his [dacha] on the Black Sea.

> K: No, but unfortunately we are going to make [Senator Henry] Jackson Secretary of Defense so you came back too late.

> D: (Laughter) No, I think it's on the contrary. [I came back] Just to congratulate him on this in time. Don't you think so?

Then later:

> K: Well, I'm delighted you're here. And you know I need not tell you that things will continue as they were.

> D: Yeah. Yes, thank you, Henry, very much.[196]

Kissinger drew a stark contrast between Nixon and Ford. Although he believed his former boss to be "one of the most gifted of American Presidents," he added that Nixon was also "obsessively incapable of overruling an interlocutor or even disagreeing with him," at

---

[196] Kissinger Transcripts. U.S. Department of State. Available at http://foia.state.gov/SearchColls/CollsSearch.asp.

least face-to-face.[197] Kissinger described never knowing for sure what Nixon would do, even after something appeared to have been decided, but under Ford "what one saw was what one got."[198] A much more self-assured man, Ford felt free to disagree and did not seem as concerned about who received the credit.[199]

Ford held his only summit with Brezhnev in November, 1974, at Vladivostok in Siberia. The different concerns of each side reflected structural differences and vulnerabilities in their respective arsenals. The Americans generally focused on Soviet land-based ICBMs, while the Soviets concentrated on American submarines and bombers. According to Soviet Foreign Minister Andrei Gromyko, Ford and Kissinger wanted the Soviets to give up a large part of their "heavy" ICBMs.[200] With their great throw weight, each one of these missiles could potentially deliver several warheads at a time. Brezhnev responded that the heavy ICBMs were essential to Soviet security because of US nuclear weapons in "forward position" in Europe.[201] The Americans continued to insist that these missiles on submarines and aircraft carriers in European waters were non-negotiable. According to Ford, "We maintained our position from previous negotiations that our Forward Base System of F-4s, F-111s and FB-111s as well as the nuclear weapons we had deployed in Western Europe not be counted in our agreed-upon total of strategic weapons."[202] Brezhnev then requested that the US stop work on the Trident submarine as well as plans to build the B-1 bomber.[203] Ford again refused, claiming "We simply couldn't rely on our aging B-52s."[204]

Nevertheless, the two sides did reach an agreement with significant arms limitations. Each superpower could have a maximum of 2,400 total strategic arms carriers, whether land, sea, or air-based and with a maximum of 1,320 equipped with MIRVs.[205] The limits would be in force from October, 1977 to December, 1985.[206] The Vladivostok Accords

---

[197] Kissinger, *Years of Renewal*, 25.

[198] Ibid.

[199] Ibid.

[200] Andrei Gromyko, *Memoirs*, translated by Harold Shukman (New York: Doubleday, 1989), 284.

[201] Ibid.

[202] Gerald Ford, *A Time to Heal* (New York: Harper & Row, 1979), 216.

[203] Ibid.

[204] Ibid.

[205] Dobrynin, *In Confidence*, 336.

[206] Ibid., 338.

thereby enshrined the principle of "absolute equality" as demanded by Jackson's amendment to SALT I in 1972.[207] However, Dobrynin believed that the Americans were never truly prepared to accept this new status quo with the Soviet Union.[208]

Although Ford and Brezhnev reached a tentative agreement on SALT II, domestic politics in both countries inhibited further progress. According to Ford, Brezhnev mentioned at Vladivostok that "some members of his Politburo didn't believe détente was a good idea."[209] Although the Politburo had attained a relative level of stability after the purges of Stalin and reorganizations under Khrushchev, this also resulted in a conservative and aged oligarchy, most of whom held lifetime positions.[210] Brezhnev was unquestionably the leader, but was also required to heed the opinions of his colleagues.[211] To complicate matters, while at the summit he suffered the first in a series of seizures signaling arteriosclerosis of the brain which would eventually prove fatal.[212] From the mid-1970s onward, Brezhnev gradually became little more than a figurehead for the regime in Moscow.[213] His declining health played right into the hands of his more hard-line opponents until his death in 1982.

Soviet politics also posed problems for Dobrynin. Some in the Party's Central Committee, the KGB, and the Foreign Ministry, perhaps jealous of his privileged position as Soviet Ambassador to the United States, accused Dobrynin of becoming too "Americanized" due to his long tenure and numerous connections in Washington.[214] The charge could have implied that Dobrynin had grown too cozy with Kissinger and therefore did not advocate sufficiently for the Soviet Union in its relations with the United States.

In the US, Kissinger observed that many of the original motivations for engaging in détente and arms control no longer existed by

---

[207] Richard W. Stevenson, *The Rise and Fall of Détente – Relaxation of Tension in US-Soviet Relations, 1953-84* (Urbana and Chicago: University of Illinois Press, 1985), 170.

[208] Dobrynin, *In Confidence*, 337.

[209] Ford, 216.

[210] Robert Strayer, *Why Did the Soviet Union Collapse? Understanding Historical Change* (Armonk, New York: M.E. Sharpe, 1998), 52.

[211] Ford, 52, 53.

[212] Dobrynin, *In Confidence*, 334.

[213] Dmitri Volkogonov, *Autopsy for an Empire – The Seven Leaders Who Built the Soviet Regime*, ed. and trans. Harold Shukman (New York: The Free Press, 1998), 324.

[214] Dobrynin, *In Confidence*, 359.

the time Ford entered office.[215] Soviet cooperation in international matters such as ending the Vietnam War, settling the question of free access to West Berlin, and restraint in the Middle East already had been largely accomplished.[216] As Kissinger put it, the main driving force for SALT II was simply to keep détente going.[217] Therefore reaching a deal did not carry the same urgency, leaving opponents less amenable to accepting a new treaty.

And there were many opponents. Liberals criticized the Vladivostok agreement because it allowed both sides to build up to the ceilings.[218] Conservatives argued that even though the Soviets had agreed to a numerical equality, they still possessed the large SS-18 missiles which had greater throw weight and could carry more warheads in a single launch.[219] Furthermore, there was the question of how to verify that each side was adhering to the treaty's limits in the first place.[220]

Technological issues also interfered with a SALT II agreement. SALT I permitted the development of new weapons, and both the US and the USSR had taken advantage of this. The Americans developed cruise missiles (which Kissinger described as "pilotless airplanes"[221]) that could fly below radar and carry nuclear weapons to their target with great accuracy – something which the Soviets wanted counted in the Vladivostok limits.[222] On the other hand, the Soviet Union possessed a new bomber dubbed "Backfire," but since it could not reach American territory, the Soviets argued that it was not technically a strategic weapon.[223] The Americans responded that if it was refueled in the air the new plane could reach the US homeland.[224] Kissinger conceded that that argument could be made for almost any plane, however.[225]

In response to political and international developments including the fall of Saigon the previous April, Ford made several major changes to his cabinet in October, 1975. The President told Vice-President Nelson

---

[215] Kissinger, *Years of Renewal*, 251.

[216] Ibid.

[217] Ibid.

[218] Ibid., 299.

[219] Ibid., 300.

[220] Garthoff, *Détente and Confrontation*, 449.

[221] Kissinger, *Years of Renewal*, 252.

[222] Dobrynin, *In Confidence*, 354.

[223] Ibid.

[224] Ibid.

[225] Kissinger, *Years of Renewal*, 301.

Rockefeller, a moderate Republican loathed by the right wing of the party, that he would not be Ford's running mate in 1976.[226] White House Chief of Staff Donald Rumsfeld replaced James Schlesinger as Secretary of Defense and George H.W. Bush, the future forty-first president, replaced William Colby as CIA director.[227] Most significantly for détente and the backchannel, Kissinger lost his post as National Security Advisor to Brent Scowcroft, but remained Secretary of State.[228] Kissinger no longer had as much access to the President nor did he chair several interdepartmental policy-making committees.[229] The "Halloween Massacre" of the cabinet including Kissinger's demotion represented Ford's attempt to distance himself from détente, and thereby mute political pressure from the right so he could focus on the general election.[230]

Thus 1976 began with no SALT II agreement in sight and with Ford facing the reality that some Americans believed détente had been an all-around foreign policy disaster. The President, who upon being appointed by Nixon to the vice-presidency humbly stated, "I'm a Ford, not a Lincoln," encountered accusations of being an accidental president who only held the office due to Nixon's resignation.[231] His need to be formally elected to the White House intensified the significance of the impending presidential election in November. Consequently, his administration stopped using the word détente in its discussions of Soviet-American relations in favor of peace through strength. In light of such developments from 1974-1976, Dobrynin referred to Vladivostok as the high point of détente, but also as the beginning of its decline.[232]

Kissinger and Dobrynin had too much invested in détente and were determined to press forward with SALT II. On January 16, 1976, they discussed plans for another Kissinger visit to Moscow:

K: I am committing political suicide going to Moscow at this time.

D: I would not go that far but I understand [the] political danger.

---

[226] Ibid., 836.

[227] Dobrynin, *In Confidence*, 355.

[228] Ibid., 356.

[229] Ibid.

[230] Kissinger, *Years of Renewal*, 838.

[231] Ibid., 17.

[232] Dobrynin, *In Confidence*, 334.

K: I am doing it because we owe it to history to try and make another effort. If we fail they will say he should not have gone and if we succeed all hell will break loose.[233]

Kissinger left for Moscow on January 19, and met Brezhnev two days later.[234] He believed Brezhnev poisoned the proceedings when in answer to a reporter's question about the recent Marxist takeover in Angola the Soviet leader "rubb[ed] our noses in our defeat" and thereby "destroyed whatever sentiment was left in the United States for agreements with the Kremlin."[235] Nevertheless, the meetings proceeded with American cruise missiles and the Soviet backfire bomber remaining issues of contention.[236] After some haggling, Kissinger and Brezhnev compromised over maximum flight ranges and numerical limitations for each.[237] Having tentatively reached a deal, the Americans and Soviets predicted a SALT II treaty later in the year.[238]

However, after a January 21 meeting of the National Security Council, the Pentagon rejected the agreement.[239] Dobrynin cited the growing tension between Secretary of Defense Rumsfeld and Kissinger as making it almost impossible for the White House to have one articulate view on SALT.[240] Former California Governor Ronald Reagan, an adamant critic of détente and arms control with the Soviet Union, further dampened chances for an arms control treaty by running against Ford in the 1976 Republican primaries.[241] In February, Ford decided that there should be no more talks on SALT II until after the election.[242] American domestic politics was preventing progress on a second arms agreement just when a new treaty became more pressing for Brezhnev's leadership due to the upcoming Communist Party Congress scheduled for later that year.[243]

---

[233] Kissinger Transcripts. U.S. Department of State.
[234] Kissinger, *Years of Renewal*, 853.
[235] Ibid., 854.
[236] Dobrynin, *In Confidence*, 368.
[237] Ibid.
[238] Stevenson, 174.
[239] Dobrynin, *In Confidence*, 369.
[240] Ibid.
[241] Stevenson, 174.
[242] Kissinger, *Years of Renewal*, 1059.
[243] Dobrynin, *In Confidence*, 356, 357.

Meanwhile, détente's critics on the right began to organize. The Committee on the Present Danger viewed the Ford administration as naïve and therefore sought to publicize what it perceived as the negative strategic consequences for the United States of the Soviet buildup.[244] Beginning with Paul Nitze, who under President Truman had helped draft the Marshall Plan to rebuild Europe after World War II, the organization grew to include former members of the Johnson, Nixon, and Ford administrations as well.[245] On March 12, 1976, Eugene V. Rostow – Under Secretary of State for Johnson, David Packard – Deputy Defense Secretary under Nixon, James Schlesinger – Ford's former Defense Secretary, and many other foreign and defense policy experts met for an organizational meeting at the Metropolitan Club in Washington, D.C.[246] Other members included anticommunist labor leaders George Meany, Jay Lovestone, and Lane Kirkland of the AFL-CIO, Rachelle Horowitz and Albert Shanker of the teachers union, John H. Lyons of the steelworkers, J.G. Turner of the engineers, and Martin Ward from the plumbers.[247] In addition to the group's founding document, "Common Sense and the Common Danger," numerous other committee papers provided intellectual ammunition for the right in general and for the presidential campaigns of Ronald Reagan in particular in 1976 and 1980.[248]

Perhaps sensing the final outcome, Kissinger and Dobrynin occasionally spoke nostalgically during the presidential campaign. At one meeting in June, Dobrynin described Kissinger as "gloomy."[249] The Secretary of State had largely lost the President's ear to Secretary of Defense Rumsfeld and the new National Security Advisor, Scowcroft. It was an unusual position for Kissinger, and as Dobrynin put it, "enforced idleness…was not his natural state."[250] In a conversation on October 29, Kissinger blamed Congress, the North Vietnamese, and the Soviets for straining détente and Soviet-American relations.[251] To which Dobrynin

---

[244] Richard Gid Powers, *Not Without Honor – The History of American Anticommunism* (New Haven: Yale University Press, 1995), 369, 370.
[245] Ibid., 367, 369.
[246] Ibid.
[247] Ibid., 370.
[248] Ibid., 367, 369.
[249] Dobrynin, *In Confidence*, 372.
[250] Ibid.
[251] Ibid., 373, 374.

replied, "'We are no saints, but neither are the Americans.'"[252] Kissinger assured his colleague that his words were merely "'a short historical excursus,'" and not meant to start an argument.[253]

Ultimately, a Kissinger-Dobrynin engineered SALT II agreement was not to be. In 1976, Jimmy Carter narrowly defeated Ford to win the presidency. The negative blowback from Ford's pardon of Nixon may have been the difference. Ford's defeat also meant the end of Henry Kissinger's tenure as Secretary of State. Likewise, it signaled the end of the eight year Kissinger-Dobrynin special relationship as it had developed in the backchannel. Nevertheless, Dobrynin called détente Kissinger's "indisputable personal achievement as a statesman."[254]

The day after the election on November 3, Dobrynin offered his condolences to Kissinger and both men pondered what might have been:

> D: I just wanted to say to you that I am going to miss you -
> - in the future I mean.

> K: I will miss you too.   If it is possible to have a Marxist friend…

> D: No problem. It was so narrow.

> K: If we had obtained a SALT agreement we would have won.

> D: That is my impression. I think it would have changed the outcome.

> K: I will stand outside the government for what I have stood for inside. You can be sure of that.

> D: I know. Perhaps we can sit down quietly sometime and talk.

> K: I would like that. I owe you an apology. Believe me I did not know what they were doing. It was inexcusable.

---

[252] Ibid., 374.

[253] Ibid.

[254] Ibid.

D: It is o.k.

K: O.K., Anatol, thank you.[255]

Kissinger's mention of an apology to Dobrynin probably stemmed from the nature of the Ford campaign. Ford felt pressure from liberals to distance himself from détente because of its association with Nixon and Watergate. Meanwhile, the charge by Reagan and other conservatives that détente had been nothing more than appeasement of the Soviet Union drove the administration to abandon even mentioning the term. For Dobrynin and Kissinger, after nearly eight years of working together a repudiation of the policy must have felt like a repudiation of them and their relationship as well.

Kissinger and Dobrynin had their greatest successes in the arms control arena for two reasons. First, both the United States and the Soviet Union agreed that reigning in the growth of nuclear weapons was a necessity and an appropriate topic for state-to-state relations. Secondly, despite the competing visions of the superpower relationship embodied in the American balance of power and Soviet correlation of forces doctrines, the transcripts revealed that Kissinger and Dobrynin each perceived that the other was well-intentioned and sincerely committed to preventing the unthinkable – nuclear war. However, when the issue was human rights – touching on the relationship between a state and its people, or foreign interventions – involving one or the other superpower and a third nation, the Americans and Soviets had radically divergent opinions as to the appropriateness of its inclusion in bilateral negotiations. These issues brought ideological differences between the Americans and Soviets into much greater focus and would test Kissinger, Dobrynin, and the fate of détente.

---

[255] Kissinger Transcripts. U.S. Department of State.

Chapter 3

Human Rights: A Diplomatic Issue or an Internal Affair?

"An attempt to transform the Soviet system – not by starting an historical process of erosion, the means we favored, but by insisting on instant conversion – was certain to be fiercely resisted by the Soviet Politburo. What are Bolsheviks if not experts in the seizure and holding of power?"[1]
-Henry Kissinger

"So the crucial difference in the Soviet and American approaches to the issue was that while the Americans wanted to export to the Soviet Union its free humanitarian and commercial values, the Soviet government simply wanted the commercial benefits of trade, but not the political values."[2]
- Anatoly Dobrynin

As with arms control, conflicting American and Soviet views of human rights complicated détente. Despite being one of the most controversial issues of the time, however, the topic appeared relatively infrequently in the Kissinger-Dobrynin telcons. While SALT, ABM, Vietnam, and the October 1973 Arab-Israeli War merited numerous and lengthy discussions, human rights conversations were relatively few and far between. Although it would be easy to conclude that neither Kissinger nor Dobrynin cared about the issue, that would be an oversimplification. In their view the central purpose of détente was to maintain peace and preserve the greatest human right – the right to life. Nevertheless, human rights ended up playing a major role in American domestic opposition to détente as well as in the Soviet response to that opposition.

The telephone transcripts show that Kissinger and Dobrynin each understood the domestic pressures and limitations faced by the other when dealing with the human rights issue. Kissinger recognized Moscow's sensitivity to discussions of internal matters, and so brought up human rights with Dobrynin somewhat reluctantly and only when necessary to improve the overall political and public atmosphere for détente. Likewise, Dobrynin sought concessions from his government on Jewish migration

---

[1] Henry Kissinger, *Years of Upheaval* (New York: Simon & Schuster, 1982), 989.
[2] Anatoly Dobrynin, *In Confidence – Moscow's Ambassador to America's Six Cold War Presidents* (New York: Times Books, 1995), 278.

and other human rights concerns due to his understanding of the issue's potential effects on American public opinion and by extension upon relaxing tensions. However, as the issue was taken out of the backchannel and public diplomacy replaced private diplomacy, it resulted in intensified repression in the short term and harm to détente in the long term.

Human Rights and Détente

The Russian people had long endured oppression. Writer and editor on Soviet affairs Abraham Brumberg noted that "the history of Russia [was] replete with struggles against tyranny – from the peasant revolts of the seventeenth and eighteenth centuries to the revolutionary outbreaks of the nineteenth and twentieth centuries."[3]   The   Russian Revolution of 1917 resulted in more of the same. "The movement for a just and classless society in Russia began with unbridled violence, denying millions of people all rights except the right to support Bolshevik policy," wrote Dmitri Volkogonov.[4] Likewise, historians with such divergent viewpoints as Richard Pipes, Sheila Fitzpatrick, and Martin Malia all agreed that the revolution leading to the birth of the Soviet state was littered with human rights atrocities.[5] This continued under Stalin when all resistance was crushed.[6]

After a period of de-Stalinization under Khrushchev, Brezhnev's regime from 1964-1982 resulted in a regression and the birth of the dissident movement. According to Robert V. Daniels, the Soviet leadership "did everything it could short of mass executions to put a lid on the expression of dissident thought," starting with the 1966 trial of writers Andrei Siniavsky and Yuli Daniel.[7] Government methods of intimidation and punishment included "selective trials and imprisonment," internal and external exile, and obstruction of educational or professional

---

[3] Abraham Brumberg, "The Rise of Dissent in the U.S.S.R.," in *In Quest of Justice – Protest and Dissent in the Soviet Union Today*, ed. Abraham Brumberg (New York: Praeger Publishers, 1970), 3.

[4] Dmitri Volkogonov, *Autopsy for an Empire – The Seven Leaders Who Built the Soviet Regime*, ed. and trans. Harold Shukman (New York: The Free Press, 1998), 1.

[5] Yanni Kotsonis, "A European Experience: Human Rights and Citizenship in Revolutionary Russia," in *Human Rights and Revolutions*, eds. Jeffrey N. Wasserstrom, Lynn Hunt, and Marilyn B. Young (Lanham, Maryland: Rowman & Littlefield Publishers, Inc., 2000), 99, n. 1.

[6] Brumberg, 3.

[7] Robert V. Daniels, *The End of the Communist Revolution* (New York: Routledge, 1993), 72.

advancement, explained Robert Strayer.[8] Although a complete return to Stalinism was not politically possible, Volkogonov claimed that Brezhnev believed in returning to some aspects of it.[9] Meanwhile Vladislav Zubok argued that the majority of the Soviet leadership in this era favored abandoning de-Stalinization and supported "greater suppression of cultural diversity, and the freezing of liberal trends in culture and art."[10] However, according to Strayer, "[h]ere and there, 'oases of open thinking' permitted some original work, even in the social sciences."[11]

By the 1970s the dissident movement stood at several thousand.[12] Although small in numbers, they developed an array of tactics to combat the Soviet regime. Chief among these was taking advantage of increased contact with the Western press as a result of détente.[13] Activists such as Aleksandr Ginzburg publicized violations of the Soviet *Constitution* and laws, as well as of international agreements like the 1948 *UN Declaration on Human Rights* and the 1975 *Helsinki Accords*.[14]

The KGB under Yuri Andropov from 1967-1982 played a key role in punishing dissidents who engaged in such activities. According to Zhores Medvedev, the Soviet security service "began to be more careful in the preparation of cases, to plant evidence, to infiltrate dissident organizations and to use more technical methods of surveillance."[15] Classifying political opponents as mentally ill and using psychiatric institutions for punishment increased as well.[16] Arnold Beichman and Mikhail S. Bernstam referred to the use of psychiatry and pharmaceuticals as "the unique achievement of the secret police during the Andropov

---

[8] Robert Strayer, *Why Did the Soviet Union Collapse? – Understanding Historical Change* (Armonk, New York: M.E. Sharpe, Inc., 1998), 54

[9] Volkogonov, 263.

[10] Vladislav Zubok, *A Failed Empire – The Soviet Union in the Cold War from Stalin to Gorbachev* (Chapel Hill: The University of North Carolina Press, 2007), 196.

[11] Strayer, 54.

[12] Nicholas Werth, "A State Against Its People: Violence, Repression, and Terror in the Soviet Union," in *The Black Book of Communism* eds. Stephane Courtois, et al., translated by Jonathan Murphy (Cambridge, Massachusetts: Harvard UniversityPress, 1999), 259.

[13] William Tompson, *The Soviet Union under Brezhnev* (London: Pearson Education Limited, 2003), 106.

[14] Ibid.

[15] Zhores Medvedev, *Andropov* (New York: W.W. Norton & Company, 1983), 64.

[16] Paul Johnson, *Modern Times – The World from the Twenties to the Nineties*. Revised ed. (New York: HarperCollins Publishers, 1991), 682.

era."[17] Thus when Andropov became General Secretary in 1982 it represented "a logical conclusion" to a period of intensified repression, according to British historian Paul Johnson.[18]

However, Brezhnevism was not Stalinism. Unlike the arbitrariness of the past, "most of the time, Brezhnev's KGB arrested people for *something* [italics in original] – if not for a genuine criminal act, then for their literary, religious, or political opposition to the Soviet system," according to Anne Applebaum.[19] In other words, dissidents in the 1970s at least "knew why they had been arrested."[20] Furthermore, Amnesty International estimated that in the mid-1970s at most ten-thousand of the one million people held in Soviet prisons were there for political crimes, a low number compared to under Stalin.[21]

The Role of Ideology

The US-Soviet conflict over human rights had a strong ideological component. Mary Hawkesworth argued that from the Soviet point of view the United States had no credibility on the issue because "the capitalist, by definition, [was] the offender of human rights."[22] Therefore, American human rights advocacy amounted to mere "deceptive propaganda," designed to destroy socialism.[23]

Furthermore according to Hawkesworth, bourgeois liberalism and Marxism-Leninism operated from different premises. Western-style liberalism evolved from natural law theory and assumed certain moral absolutes including the inherent value of all people.[24] On the other hand, Marxism-Leninism argued that morals were relative. The theory rejected Western values because it considered them to be mere creations of the property-owning class (bourgeoisie) as a means of protecting its dominant position in society.[25] Writing of the bourgeoisie, communism's founders Marx and Engels argued:

---

[17] Arnold Beichman and Mikhail S. Bernstam, *Andropov – New Challenge to the West* (New York: Stein and Day Publishers, 1983), 182.

[18] Johnson, 683.

[19] Anne Applebaum, *Gulag – A History* (New York: Doubleday, 2003), 528.

[20] Ibid.

[21] Ibid.

[22] Mary Hawkesworth, "Ideological Immunity: The Soviet Response to Human Rights Criticism," *Universal Human Rights*, Vol. 2, No. 1 (Jan.-Mar., 1980), 69.

[23] Ibid., 69, 84.

[24] Ibid., 69-70.

[25] Ibid., 70.

Your very ideas are but the outgrowth of the conditions of your bourgeois production and bourgeois property, just as your jurisprudence is but the will of your class made into a law for all, a will whose essential character and direction are determined by the economical conditions of existence of your class.[26]

In essence, the Marxist-Leninist viewed Western notions of human rights as illegitimate because they emanated from class-based societies, and as long as classes existed there could be neither freedom nor equality.[27]

In contrast to the American notion of unalienable natural rights granted from the Creator as expressed in the *Declaration of Independence* (1776), the Soviet *Constitution* of 1977 espoused what Hawkesworth called "the contingency of rights," based upon whether an individual did work beneficial to all of society.[28] Only those who did such work could enjoy economic rights like food, clothing, shelter, work, rest, and education, which the Soviets prioritized above American political rights such as freedom of speech, the press, and religion.[29]

Also citing ideological considerations was Geoffrey Edwards, rapporteur to the Helsinki Review Group – monitors of compliance with the 1975 *Helsinki Accords* on human rights. He claimed that the Soviet *Constitution* contained "an uneasy dualism" between the rights of the individual and those of the state.[30] In general, the West believed that when conflicts arose between the individual and the state, the rights of the former must prevail, whereas the East favored the latter, he added.[31] While the Soviet *Constitution* did list specific individual rights, it stipulated that the interests of the party and state took precedence. Additionally, rights were "'inseparable'" from "'duties and obligations.'"[32] Although the Soviet *Constitution* guaranteed equality for all citizens, the exception made for political opponents of the state

---

[26] Karl Marx and Friedrich Engels, *The Communist Manifesto*, trans. Samuel Moore (New York: Pocket Books, 1964), 87.

[27] Hawkesworth, 70.

[28] Ibid., 72.

[29] Ibid.

[30] Geoffrey Edwards, "Human Rights and Basket III Issues: Areas of Change and Continuity," *International Affairs* (Royal Institute of International Affairs 1944-), Vol. 61, No. 4 (Autumn, 1985), 632.

[31] Ibid.

[32] Ibid.

rendered this provision as well as the human rights protections of the *Helsinki Accords* essentially meaningless.[33] "In a people's state, it would seem, only enemy agents, criminals and the insane could be opposed to the system," wrote Edwards.[34]

Jewish Emigration

In the 1970s American Jewish activists began pressuring the Soviet Union to alter its emigration policies, which Dobrynin believed did more damage to détente than any other issue.[35] According to him, "Jewish extremist groups" picketed the Soviet embassy on nearly a daily basis and Soviet offices in Washington and New York were exposed to explosions and rifle shots.[36] Privately, Jewish leaders and the White House condemned such actions by groups including Meir Kahane's Jewish Defense League.[37] Dobrynin also credited the US State Department for providing security and recommending Soviet diplomats and their families exercise extreme caution.[38]

Emigration embarrassed the Soviets because it suggested that communism had failed to create the ideal society. Kissinger understood this well. For his part, Dobrynin knew the saliency of human rights to the American public. By opting for quiet diplomacy both could feel free to reply to each other's requests on emigration and other issues favorably without appearing to "capitulate."[39] Kissinger described how he and Dobrynin handled the issue privately:

> No formal requests were made, and no formal responses were given. Soviet actions were noted without being acknowledged. Indeed, the emigration practices of the Soviet Union were steadily improving, though no claim to that effect was ever made by Washington. The Nixon Administration stuck to these ground rules so meticulously

---

[33] Ibid., 632, 633.

[34] Ibid., 633.

[35] Dobrynin, *In Confidence*, 339.

[36] Ibid., 271.

[37] Ibid.

[38] Ibid., 271, 272.

[39] Sandy Vogelgesang, "Diplomacy of Human Rights," *International Studies Quarterly* Vol. 23, No. 2, Special Issue on Human Rights (Jun. 1979): 220.

that it never claimed any credit for improving Soviet emigration practices-even during election campaigns-...,"[40]

As détente's fortunes flourished via the Kissinger-Dobrynin backchannel, so did those of Soviet Jews wishing to emigrate. From 1970-1973 the numbers increased steadily: 1,000 in 1970, 15,000 in 1971, 30,000 in 1972, and finally 35,000 in 1973.[41] The 65,000 emigrants from 1972-1973 corresponded to when détente was at its height.[42] Moscow's change in policy probably resulted from several factors including a desire for a "safety valve" to release pressure from a "disaffected but homogenous" group of citizens.[43] The expectation that Washington would reciprocate with some future gesture of its own could have also played a part.[44] Nevertheless, many Soviet Jews continued to suffer from delays, harassment, and refusals.[45]

Jewish Emigrants from the Soviet Union, 1970-1975

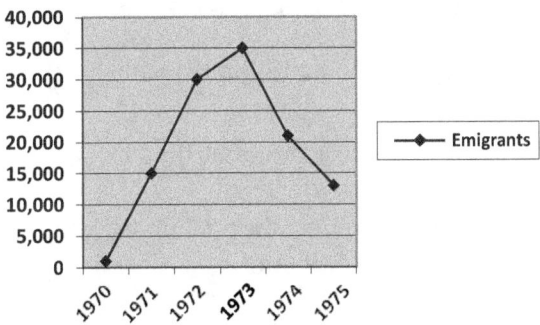

However, if the issue arose outside of the backchannel then Kissinger and Dobrynin handled it quite differently. When a staff member brought a letter calling attention to the plight of Soviet Jews directly to

---

[40] Henry Kissinger, *Diplomacy* (New York: Simon & Schuster, 1994), 753.

[41] Richard W. Stevenson, *The Rise and Fall of Détente – Relaxations of Tension in US-Soviet Relations, 1954-84* (Urbana and Chicago: University of Illinois Press, 1985), 162.

[42] Adam B. Ulam, *Dangerous Relations – The Soviet Union in World Politics, 1970-1982* (New York: Oxford University Press, 1983), 81.

[43] Harry Gelman, *The Brezhnev Politburo and the Decline of Détente* (Ithaca: Cornell University Press, 1984), 147.

[44] Ibid.

[45] Ulam, 82.

Nixon, Dobrynin expressed his concern to Kissinger. After some investigation, the following discussion occurred on February 15, 1972:

> K: ...I have looked into this matter of the letter about the Jewish problem.
>
> D: Yes.
>
> K: There is no consolation in the result, but I can assure you it was the result of an overeager staff man who brought it in without explaining what it was about. I can tell you privately that the President is extremely angry.
>
> D: I don't care about the specifics of it.
>
> K: I just wanted you to know. If we want to needle you, we will find another way to do it.
>
> D: It creates some publicity which goes back home.
>
> K: You let your people know about this.
>
> D: I would like it not to happen in the future. In this particular case, it doesn't matter.
>
> K: It will not happen in the future without my telling you first.[46]

Kissinger's embarrassment as well as Dobrynin's annoyance at what they both viewed as a violation of diplomatic etiquette was readily apparent. They had an understanding that such issues would be handled privately, through the backchannel. Kissinger assured Dobrynin that in the future he would notify him of anything posing such potential negative publicity. However, "the Jewish problem" was not going away.

Based upon an agreement signed by Nixon and Brezhnev at the June, 1972 Moscow summit, the *Trade Reform Act of 1972* held

---

[46] [September 1971-April 1972. Box #27.] *Henry A. Kissinger Telephone Conversation Transcripts (Telcons): [Anatoly Dobrynin File]*. Richard Nixon Presidential Library and Museum, Yorba Linda, California. National Archives and Records Administration.

numerous potential benefits for both superpowers. The USSR would obtain Most Favored Nation (MFN) trading status and thereby benefit from lower tariffs on Russian imports including vodka, while the US would finally receive $722 million owed from the World War II lend-lease program.[47]

Although MFN only provided the same trading benefits which over one hundred other nations enjoyed, Kissinger believed that to the Soviets it conferred legitimacy, respect, and above all, equality.[48] Nixon and Kissinger also calculated that MFN could be offered as a *quid pro quo* in exchange for Soviet restraint internationally.[49] Both countries would prosper from a greater exchange of goods, with the added benefit for the US of increasing democracy's influence behind the Iron Curtain.[50]

However, on August 3 Moscow began charging a 25,000 exit tax on emigrants.[51] The Soviets justified the tax as a means to reimburse the government for educational expenses.[52] Once again, Kissinger's nemesis Senator Jackson entered the debate. On October 4 he and seventy-one co-sponsors introduced an amendment to the trade bill.[53] What would become known as the *Jackson-Vanik Amendment* mandated that the United States would only award MFN status to countries with non-market based economies provided that they removed their emigration restrictions.[54] The intent behind the legislation was primarily to force the Soviet Union to allow its Jewish citizens to leave the country. Democratic Representative Charles Vanik of Ohio introduced his corresponding bill in the House on October 10.[55]

The White House had no official comment on the tax.[56] However, the public had much to say. Special consultant to the president on Israel and Jewish affairs Leonard Garment told Kissinger, "The Russian issue is

---

[47] Yanek Mieczkowski, *Gerald Ford and the Challenges of the 1970s* (Lexington, Kentucky: The University Press of Kentucky, 2005), 278.

[48] Kissinger, *Diplomacy*, 753-754.

[49] Mieczkowski, 278.

[50] Ibid.

[51] Stevenson, 162; Robert Dallek, *Nixon and Kissinger–Partners in Power* (New York: HarperCollins Publishers, 2007), 413.

[52] Keith L. Nelson, *The Making of Détente – Soviet American Relations in the Shadow of Vietnam* (Baltimore: The Johns Hopkins Press, 1995), 118.

[53] Kissinger, *White House Years* (New York: Simon & Schuster, 1979), 1272.

[54] Kissinger, *Years of Upheaval*, 250.

[55] Ibid., 251.

[56] Dallek, 413.

flooding my desk."[57] Kissinger called the American Jewish community "self-serving."[58] To him *Jackson-Vanik* represented a cynical attempt to "extend the conventional criticism of Nixon's alleged moral insensitivity into new areas of policy, including foreign affairs, in which Nixon's competence had heretofore gone unchallenged."[59]

To Dobrynin, the amendment was part of "a vitriolic but politically sophisticated campaign" which damaged American-Soviet relations from then on.[60] However, he also could not understand why his government would not remove its restrictions on Jewish emigration. He believed that doing so would have eliminated a persistent source of conflict with the West and particularly the Americans.[61] He also claimed that the Politburo never gave a reasonable answer when queried privately on the issue.[62] Some Soviet leaders held to Stalin's view of emigrants as traitors, others argued that Jews had knowledge of state secrets due to their work in scientific fields, and some feared that increased Jewish emigration would alienate Moscow's allies in the Arab world.[63] Indeed, the Kremlin was probably eager to return to the good graces of Egypt in particular after its president, Anwar Sadat, expelled all Soviet troops in July.[64] However, with remarkable candor Dobrynin opined that the real reason for restricting Jewish emigration derived from Moscow's fear "of emigration in general (irrespective of nationality or religion) lest an escape hatch from the happy land of socialism seem to offer a degree of liberalization that might destabilize the domestic situation."[65]

Ultimately, the answer to the mystery of the exit tax may lie with Politburo member and Chief Party Ideologist Mikhail Suslov. According to biographer Serge Petroff, "Suslov continued to remind the leadership that the Soviet Union had an ideological rather than a national basis for its existence."[66] Consequently, even at a state of détente Suslov tended to advocate for an increased emphasis on the ideological struggle with the

---

[57] Ibid.

[58] Ibid.

[59] Kissinger, *Years of Upheaval*, 251.

[60] Dobrynin, *In Confidence*, 272.

[61] Ibid.

[62] Ibid.

[63] Ibid.

[64] Nelson, 118.

[65] Dobrynin, *In Confidence*, 273.

[66] Serge Petroff, *The Red Eminence – A Biography of Mikhail A. Suslov* (Clifton, New Jersey: The Kingston Press, Inc., 1988), 184.

West in order to inoculate the Soviet Union from the corrupting effects of greater Western contact.[67] Dobrynin reported that Suslov had been left in charge in Moscow while Brezhnev and Gromyko were vacationing on the Black Sea.[68] He suspected that Suslov personally opposed both détente and relaxing emigration rules and so agreed to the tax.[69]

Despite Kissinger's and Dobrynin's previous success in the backchannel, Senator Jackson would not be satisfied with quiet diplomacy when it came to human rights – he believed that American advocacy should be public and unambiguous.[70] Dobrynin claimed that Jackson sought victory over the Soviets in order to further his political career.[71] Meanwhile Kissinger called it a "pity" that although the White House and the Senator had the same goals on emigration, they could not agree upon the same "tactics."[72] Regardless of how well-intentioned he may have been, Jackson undoubtedly had political motives as well for introducing his amendment. In addition to attracting Jewish votes in his home state, he had plans to run for president in 1976.[73] Likewise, co-sponsor Vanik served many Jewish constituents in his Cleveland, Ohio congressional district.[74]

With the controversy intensifying, Treasury Secretary George Schultz (a future Secretary of State under Reagan) was scheduled to visit Moscow in the spring of 1973 for talks on expanding trade. On March 12, Dobrynin and Kissinger discussed the visit as well as the need to keep talk of Jewish emigration quiet because of its potentially detrimental effects on détente:

> D: You know, we could discuss right now why I decided to call you, not because of the situation, but chiefly I received a telegram from Brezhnev in connection with [what] you asked about Shultz [sic].

---

[67] Dimitri K. Simes, *Détente and Conflict: Soviet Foreign Policy, 1972-1977*, The Center for Strategic and International Studies, Georgetown University, Washington, D.C. (Beverly Hills: Sage Publications, 1977), 58, 59.
[68] Dobrynin, *In Confidence*, 273.
[69] Ibid.
[70] Kissinger, *Diplomacy*, 754.
[71] Dobrynin, *In Confidence*, 275.
[72] Kissinger, *Years of Upheaval*, 254.
[73] Mieczkowksi, 278.
[74] Ibid.

K: Yeah.

D: he just ask[ed] me to tell you that definitely he is going to receive Shultz.

K: That's a good idea.

D: So, you may be sure that Brezhnev will receive Shultz. And he said to me, I told you so, so what is the question.

K: Evidently, Anatol, it might be just as well if you didn't raise the Jewish question with Shultz.

D: Don't raise with Shultz.

K: Don't raise it, because, unless there is something positive you want to say, because if you do raise and then you see, he is not quite as devious as I am, he may report something honestly which causes us trouble with the Congress.

D: I see, okay.[75]

As the Treasury Secretary making an official visit, Schultz operated outside of the backchannel and could be called upon to comment publicly or even testify before Congress about his trip. Kissinger's concern for avoiding any public mention of Jewish emigration led him to ask Dobrynin to not bring up the subject with Schultz. While one could question the ethics of conducting foreign policy in this manner, it demonstrated how Kissinger understood Soviet sensitivity vis-à-vis their domestic policies. It also showed both men's dedication to quiet diplomacy in order to protect detente.

As the White House sought a compromise with the Senate on MFN, Dobrynin persistently inquired about its progress. On March 17, Kissinger explained that he could see the light at the end of the tunnel, provided that he had Dobrynin's permission to pass on a letter to the senators specifying proposed Soviet compromises:

---

[75] [March 1973. Box #27.]

K: Well, on the MFN I can already answer.

D: Yes, what is answer.

K: We think it will go through the House in the first week of August.

D: I see.

K: And in the Senate, oh, sometime during October we think.

Then later…

K: We can give them the text you gave us[?]

D: I think it is better to say, not to give them the text.

K: Not to give it. Just to read it.

D: I think you can give just a summary, that's all.

K: Okay, fine.[76]

Although willing to deliver concessions on emigration, perhaps even tentatively agreeing to a certain amount of exit visas to be granted annually, Dobrynin resisted putting them in writing, perhaps out of fear that the information could leak. The Soviet Union did not want it to appear as if thousands of its citizens desired to leave the country, even if it was true.

Initially it appeared to the White House that the exit tax alone had caused the controversy.[77] Remove the tax, and you removed the problem. On March 30, Dobrynin delivered a private message from the Soviet leadership to Kissinger asserting that emigration was an internal affair and criticizing the "'noisy campaign'" which was "'artificial and ill-meaning.'"[78]   Nevertheless, the Soviets would end the emigration tax

---

[76] Ibid.

[77] Kissinger, *Years of Upheaval*, 252.

[78] Ibid.

except for certain circumstances related to security concerns.[79] On April 16, Kissinger and Dobrynin agreed on the exact wording of a statement announcing the suspension of the exit tax which was then submitted to Congress.[80]

Two days later, Nixon announced at the White House that the Soviets had agreed to drop the exit tax for Soviet Jews wishing to immigrate to Israel.[81] However, Kissinger alleged that due to the brewing Watergate scandal Congress was not in the mood for compromise.[82] Indeed, several politicians may have already smelled blood in the water and been thinking ahead to the 1974 Congressional mid-term elections. However, the White House did not help itself by excluding Congress from negotiations with the Kremlin over the issue.[83] Consequently, Jackson and numerous others increased their demands to include a guaranteed minimum number of exit visas and eased emigration restrictions for all Soviet citizens, not just Jews.[84] According to Dobrynin, this suggested that the number of people wishing to leave the Soviet Union was endless.[85] Such an implication could only be taken extremely negatively by Moscow.

The White House remained undeterred. The commitment to obtaining MFN for the Soviets was such that Nixon had Kissinger tell Israeli Prime Minister Golda Meir to stay out of the debate.[86] On April 22 Kissinger discussed with Dobrynin a recent conversation he had held with the Israeli ambassador:

D: …you said that you spoke with the Ambassador about this—

K: Oh, oh, well, I told the Ambassador that we would take very serious measures if they obstructed MFN. And between you and me, even going to airplane deliveries.

---

[79] Ibid.

[80] Ibid., 253.

[81] Stevenson, 162.

[82] Kissinger, *Years of Upheaval*, 253.

[83] Stevenson, 162.

[84] Kissinger, *Years of Upheaval*, 253- 254.

[85] Dobrynin, *In Confidence*, 274.

[86] Ibid.

D: That you mentioned him directly this way?

K: Yeah. I mean, don't publish this.

D: No, Henry. But did you ever see anything published which we discuss with you?

K: No.

D: I don't know anything we have.

K: No, but I mean, we were very tough. And if you could see the reaction of the Jewish leaders, I think that it was not uninfluenced by them.

D: All right, Henry.

K: We will push it through, Anatol.[87]

Kissinger's statement to the Israeli ambassador was probably not an idle threat. When war broke out between the Arabs and Israelis that October, the White House did not respond with an immediate airlift out of concern that such a move would hurt Washington's role as a peacemaker thereafter. Furthermore, when the Israelis later appeared to be advancing on Cairo en route to a total victory, Nixon and Kissinger compelled them to withdraw. Consequently, it seems highly likely that Kissinger would indeed punish Tel Aviv if they interfered with MFN. Not even the protests of America's most important strategic ally in the Middle East would stop Kissinger from coming through for Dobrynin on this prime carrot of détente.

The second Nixon-Brezhnev summit was held in May, 1973, in Washington as well as at Nixon's "Western White House" in San Clemente, California. Dobrynin blamed the MFN-emigration controversy in part for the failure of this second meeting to advance American-Soviet economic ties.[88]

---

[87] [April 1973. Box #27.]

[88] Dobrynin, *In Confidence*, 275.

Meanwhile, negotiations continued in the backchannel. On July 3, Kissinger spoke to Dobrynin from San Clemente.[89] While in California, several prominent Jewish leaders had asked to visit with him, but Kissinger insisted on meeting in Washington instead.[90] Kissinger sought Dobrynin's help in obtaining emigration concessions to relay to the Jewish leaders at a forthcoming meeting in order to rally support for MFN:

> HK: And you see frankly if there is anything…that I could tell them then it would be worth seeing them and it would help with the legislation.

> AD: I think it would be better to delay it when you will be back here.

> HK: Well, I'll certainly—I tell you now I will not see them here, because I don't want to create the impression that we are having a special meeting that requires a long trip…I'm wondering Anatol whether you could find out for me by the time I get back next week whether there is anything at all that I can say…

> AD: Okay, I check with him [Brezhnev] once more, but now he is in Moscow—I will check with him and what he really has in mind…[91]

About two weeks later on the 19th, Dobrynin responded to a query by Kissinger concerning a list of Jewish families which had been passed along to the Soviets:

> D: …this is answer about the question you raise yesterday. First about this list of some Jewish families.

> K: Yes.

> D: …the final decision is not yet taken because they vote one way or another over security restrictions.

---

[89] [July 1973-September 1973. Box #28.]

[90] Ibid.

[91] Ibid.

K: How many?

D: More than 80. Around 80 or 90, something like that. They are now – their applications are being considered in the light of developments.

K: Can I say that? Oh, that explains the discrepancy in numbers?

D: You may say, but it is not decided whether they will give them permission or not. So this is the only thing I could tell, but you may say[92]

The Soviets often refused visas to citizens on the basis of security restrictions. How legitimate these claims were was debatable, but what is clear is that détente drove the Politburo to consider such requests in much greater numbers than ever before.

The next Congressional session brought more developments. On September 14, 1973, Andrei Sakharov – dissident, physicist, and father of the Soviet hydrogen bomb –sent an impassioned letter to the US Congress urging passage of *Jackson-Vanik*:

...there are tens of thousands of citizens in the Soviet Union – Jews, Germans, Russians, Ukrainians, Lithuanians, Armenians, Estonians Latvians, Turks and members of other ethnic groups – who want to leave the country and who have been seeking to exercise that right for years and for decades at the cost of endless difficulty and humiliation. You know that prisons, labor camps, and mental hospitals are full of people who have sought to exercise this legitimate right.[93]

Then in a refutation of the Kissinger-Dobrynin approach, Sakharov added that "'quiet diplomacy'" could only help "a few individuals in Moscow and some other cities."[94] Finally, he called on "the Congress of the United

---

[92] Ibid.

[93] Andrei Sakharov, "A Letter to the Congress of the United States," in *Sakharov Speaks*, ed. Harrison A. Salisbury (New York: Alfred A. Knopf, 1974), 212-213.

[94] Ibid., 214.

States, reflecting the will and the traditional love of freedom of the American people," to pass the amendment.[95] About two weeks later on the 27th, historian Arthur M. Schlesinger, Jr. wrote a piece for the *Wall Street Journal* explaining that although he supported increased US-Soviet trade, Sakharov's endorsement of *Jackson-Vanik* had swayed him.[96] "'Always trust the man on the firing line,'" wrote Schlesinger.[97]

The October, 1973 Arab-Israeli/Yom Kippur War temporarily placed the trade bill on the back-burner. Moscow's desire for MFN led the Soviets to continue allowing Jewish emigration over the objections of the Arabs.[98] However, the Soviet role in arming the Egyptians and Syrians against Israel may have provided Jackson with the added encouragement and support from the public he needed in order to continue pushing for his amendment.[99]

On December 11, the *Jackson-Vanik Amendment* easily passed in the House 319 to 80.[100] On the 26th Nixon relayed to Dobrynin his "profound contempt" for the "liberals, Zionists, and conservatives" who had blocked MFN.[101] "We must not let temporary setbacks, no matter how discouraging, interfere with or poison the relations between the two superpowers," he added.[102] The next stop was the Senate, and if it did as well there Congress would have more than enough votes to override a presidential veto.

By 1974, the controversy over Jewish emigration had held up the trade bill for over a year. After being armed by Dobrynin with the latest Soviet statistics on Jewish emigration, Kissinger met with Jackson on March 6.[103] Kissinger proposed a compromise whereby the Soviets would receive MFN, but the Senate would have the right to review Moscow's emigration policies on a regular basis.[104] Jackson rejected the idea,

---

[95] Ibid., 215.

[96] Kissinger, *Years of Upheaval*, 988.

[97] Ibid.

[98] Raymond L. Garthoff, *Détente and Confrontation: American-Soviet Relations from Nixon to Reagan* (Washington, D.C.: Brookings Institution, 1985), 396.

[99] Nelson, 147.

[100] Richard Nixon, *RN – The Memoirs of Richard Nixon* (New York: Grosset & Dunlap, 1978), 876; Kissinger, *Years of Upheaval*, 991.

[101] Nixon, 875, 876.

[102] Ibid., 876.

[103] Kissinger, *Years of Upheaval*, 991.

[104] Ibid., 992, 993.

instead insisting on a written guarantee of dramatic increases in emigration.[105]

After months of further negotiations, Kissinger phoned Dobrynin on June 5 to report that he might have a deal with Jackson as well as Democratic Senators Jacob Javits of New York and Abraham Ribicoff of Connecticut. When it took several rings before Dobrynin answered, Kissinger could not resist one of his verbal jabs:

> K: There's almost no sense tapping you anymore if you
> don't pick it up.[!]
> I had breakfast this morning with Jackson, Javits and
> Ribicoff. You know, it's a little premature, but I think we
> will be successful.
>
> D: Along what lines?
>
> K: Along the lines we discussed yesterday.
>
> D: For trade?
>
> K: For trade and credits.
>
> D: Along what lines?
>
> K: Well, the 45,000.
>
> D: 45?
>
> K: Well, the number…
>
> D: Oh, you mean about this…
>
> K: Jewish question.

Then later:

---

[105] Ibid., 993.

K: ...he will modify his amendments so that MFN is possible and credits will not be restricted. You know with a review maybe every year.

D: I understand. When we meet next time you are going to show me this letter.

K: I will not send the letter without discussing it with you.

D: OK. In one way or the other it's better to get rid of all these issues.[106]

Dobrynin's patience was clearly growing thin. However, Kissinger believed he had finally reached a compromise with Jackson and the other senators whereby the Soviets would get MFN, but the Senate would retain the right to an annual review based upon emigration statistics. The agreement would be summarized in a letter to Jackson, which Kissinger would give Dobrynin an opportunity to preview. Consequently, there would be no surprises or misunderstandings.

Despite their best efforts, circumstances continued to work against Kissinger and Dobrynin. On June 30 the President's ability to use export-import bank credits came up for Congressional renewal.[107] Senators Adlai Stevenson III of Illinois, Jackson, and eighteen others proceeded to introduce the *Stevenson Amendment* placing a $300 million limit on all US export-import bank loans to the Soviet Union with any loan over $50 million being subject to a possible review.[108] The final version of the amendment prohibited the use of funds for development and energy as well.[109]

The *Jackson* and *Stevenson* amendments were draining Moscow's incentive for cooperating on human rights issues. Even if the Soviets met the Senate's numbers on emigration and thereby obtained MFN, the amount of money they could borrow for trade would be tightly

---

[106] Kissinger Transcripts. U.S. Department of State. Available at http://foia.state.gov/SearchColls/CollsSearch.asp.
[107] Kissinger, *Years of Upheaval*, 996.
[108] Richard C. Thornton, *The Nixon-Kissinger Years – The Reshaping of American Foreign Policy*, 2nd ed. (St. Paul, Minnesota: Paragon House, 2001), 321.
[109] Gelman, 148.

controlled.[110] If the White House could deliver neither MFN nor credits to the Soviets, Nixon and Kissinger would be without two of their main instruments for conducting détente. In Kissinger's view, by this time "[the] carrot had for all practical purposes ceased to exist."[111]

On August 9, 1974, Gerald Ford became the thirty-eighth President of the United States after the Watergate affair forced Nixon to resign. According to Gates, one of the things the Soviets liked most about working with Nixon and Kissinger was that they "never tried to cause the Soviets trouble at home, to question seriously their internal policies or the legitimacy of their rule."[112] However, after Nixon exited Gates saw a shift in US policy.[113] This probably had little to do with any changes implemented by Ford. Due to Vietnam and the Watergate scandal, power in Washington had been moving steadily away from the presidency and toward Congress for at least a year by this time and would continue to do so throughout the 1970s.

On August 14, Dobrynin gave Ford an "unwritten guarantee" that 50,000 Soviet Jews would be permitted to emigrate every year.[114] (Ford stated that the figure was 55,000).[115] Dobrynin refused to put it in writing due to fear that Jackson would use the information for political propaganda.[116] The next day, the President attempted to break the impasse over *Jackson-Vanik* and MFN by inviting Jackson, Javits, and Ribicoff to the Oval Office for breakfast.[117] Ford relayed Dobrynin's assurances and Jackson reciprocated by lowering his demand to 75,000 after having been as high as 100,000.[118]

Although Javits and Ribicoff were satisfied with Dobrynin's word, Jackson still insisted that any guarantee had to be in writing.[119] According to Ford, Jackson accused the White House of "being too soft on the

---

[110] Kissinger, *Years of Upheaval*, 997.

[111] Ibid., 998.

[112] Robert M. Gates, *From the Shadows – The Ultimate Insider's Story of Five Presidents and How They Won the Cold War* (New York: Simon & Schuster, 1996), 85.

[113] Ibid.

[114] Henry Kissinger, *Years of Renewal* (New York: Simon & Schuster, 1999), 256; Dobrynin, *In Confidence*, 339.

[115] Gerald Ford, *A Time to Heal* (New York: Harper & Row, 1979), 138.

[116] Ibid.

[117] Kissinger, *Years of Renewal*, 256; Ford, 139.

[118] Kissinger, *Years of Renewal*, 256.

[119] Dobrynin, *In Confidence*, 340.

Russians."[120] Nevertheless, they finally reached a deal on October 18 whereby the Senator would alter his legislation based upon an "understanding" that the Soviets would provide 60,000 exit visas annually.[121]

Jackson, who of course had presidential aspirations, felt compelled to make the news public. When he announced the deal before the press on the White House lawn, the Soviets were outraged.[122] Kissinger told Dobrynin that the President was furious with Jackson, even going so far as to say that the Senator had "'behaved like a swine.'"[123] Although the White House later explained that the Soviets had never agreed to an exact number, the damage had been done.[124]

Things began to move quickly. On December 3 Kissinger testified before the Senate Finance Committee.[125] He stressed that the Soviets had not committed to a definite number of actual Jewish emigrants.[126] Nevertheless, on the 13th the Senate passed the trade bill with the amendments, 77-4.[127] After ironing out differences in the conference committee, on December 20 the bill went to the White House.[128] Ford signed it into law on January 3, 1975, and praised it for the economic benefits to both countries, but also criticized the legislation for conditions and restrictions uniquely placed upon the Soviet Union.[129] The President revealed that he never seriously considered a veto because the legislation had passed both houses comfortably.[130]

With the passage of *Jackson-Vanik*, for the first time the United States of America had passed legislation promoting international human rights.[131] It was a significant milestone. However, the Soviets were unimpressed. On January 10, Dobrynin delivered a private statement to

---

[120] Ford, 139.

[121] Garthoff, *Détente and Confrontation*, 455; Ulam, 123.

[122] Garthoff, *Détente and Confrontation*, 455, 456.

[123] Dobrynin, *In Confidence*, 340.

[124] Kissinger, *Years of Renewal*, 259.

[125] Ibid., 303.

[126] Ibid., 304.

[127] Garthoff, *Détente and Confrontation*, 459.

[128] Ford, 225.

[129] Kissinger, *Years of Renewal*, 306.

[130] Ford, 225.

[131] Jay Winik, *On the Brink – The Dramatic, Behind-the-Scenes Saga of the Reagan Era and the Men and Women Who Won the Cold War* (New York: Simon & Schuster, 1996), 57.

Kissinger explaining that Moscow was rejecting Congress's conditions and cancelling the trade agreement altogether.[132]

Kissinger was confused by Dobrynin's statement. It sounded to him as if the Soviets were not merely repudiating the trade agreement, but also détente and everything for which he and Dobrynin had been working. On January 13, Kissinger sought a clarification, but Dobrynin's response only added to his fears:

> K: The one thing that concerns me is that you keep making references to - - that you are freed of your obligations in 1972. I don't know what obligations you are talking about.
>
> D: There are several things there…they consider as it was for three years - - unconditional so they consider to terminate it as it is. So it is probably needed to be discussed at a later date of course between our agencies who deal with the trade one-by-one. We didn't go into the details because you know under the '72 as you remember - - it's for three years.
>
> K: But only those items that were covered in the trade agreement. I mean you don't mean for example the maritime agreement.
>
> D: No, no. Only the trade agreement.
>
> K: Okay.
>
> D: So this is within the…..
>
> K: *You are not denouncing the SALT agreement?*
>
> D: *Well, well, I think we will come to that one on a later date - - no, no, I am joking.*[133] (italics mine)

---

[132] Kissinger, *Years of Renewal*, 306.

[133] Kissinger Transcripts. U.S. Department of State.

This was a most curious exchange. Kissinger was unclear where the Soviets now stood on détente. Inexplicably, Dobrynin at first saw fit to make a joke and let Kissinger believe the worst. Could this have been a Freudian slip, revealing such disgust amongst the Soviet leadership that they had considered abandoning détente? Moscow must have been thoroughly fed up with the American legislative process by this point. The delay in getting SALT I ratified had been bad enough, but this time the Kremlin found Jackson's interference in its *internal* affairs to be intolerable.

Dobrynin quickly changed the subject to whether or not President Ford would publicly condemn Congress's action:

> D: Will the President [lead?] with this in general in his own statement or he will just only give domestic affairs mostly, I mean on Wednesday.

> K: I think the President will not mention it specifically but I will give a speech next week in which I will hit it very hard.

> D: Where are you going to make it?

> K: In Los Angeles.

> D: Oh, in Los Angeles.

> K: Assuming you don't keep attacking me in Pravda.

> D: On the contrary. A special concession after which everybody will listen with special care.

> K: Okay, Anatol.[134]

Kissinger's speech would not criticize the Soviets for disavowing the trade agreement, but attack *Congress* for its actions, which he believed had prompted a diplomatic catastrophe. Dobrynin seemed somewhat disappointed that Kissinger would not be condemning the bill from

---

[134] Ibid.

Washington, thereby denying the speech an official imprimatur. Nevertheless, he seemed satisfied with Kissinger's reaction. As usual, Kissinger told Dobrynin that he could review the official State Department response to the Soviet withdrawal before anything was said publicly.[135] Despite a massive setback for détente, both men sought to maintain the relationship as before.

That was not the end of the controversy. On February 3, 1975, Kissinger phoned *New York Times* publisher Punch Sulzberger to furiously protest a column by William Safire. A former Nixon speechwriter, Safire had left the administration and later discovered that he was one of many who had been wiretapped in an effort to uncover leaks.[136] The column alleged that Kissinger and Dobrynin had conspired to cancel the trade agreement due to the passage of the *Jackson-Vanik* and *Stevenson* amendments. In doing so, the Soviets would avoid capitulating on Jewish emigration while the White House could benefit politically by blaming Congress for interfering with foreign policy. Unable to reach Sulzberger, Kissinger phoned editor John Oakes, who attempted to calm down the still-irate Secretary of State:

> K: ...now today Saffire [sic] accuses the Secretary of State of colluding with a Soviet Ambassador for domestic political gain on an issue which again I [initiated?] the whole thing of moving emigration before Jackson was ever heard of. It's unbelievable that this sort of thing can happen.

> O: I have to tell you, I think the Saffire thing was really outrageous myself...I want you to know the publisher [Sulzberger] came down stairs to see me and we talked about it in another office.

Then later...

> K: ...no [matter how] much I would oppose a Congressional action, the idea that the Secretary of State could collude with a Soviet Ambassador is unbelievable.

---

[135] Ibid.

[136] William Safire, "The Suspicious 17; Essay," *New York Times*, 9 August 1973.

O: I just cannot defend and have no intention of defending the Saffire piece. I just have to say to you what is the absolute truth and what Punch has already said. The columnist[s] are absolutely independent.

K: OK. I made my protest and there's nothing you can do about it.

O: I'm really thinking out loud. Is there anything you would want to state for publication.

K: I don't think the Secretary of State should write a letter saying *no, I did not collude with the Soviet Ambassador.*[137] (italics mine)

Safire obviously had his own personal reasons for being resentful towards Kissinger. Whether or not there was any truth to the allegation, the fact that the former speech writer could charge Kissinger and Dobrynin with collusion was revealing. After six years of working together, there may have been the perception in Washington (as well as in Moscow) that they had become too close. Inevitably, this aroused suspicions among certain circles on both sides, and combined with Kissinger's reputation for practicing *realpolitik*, the possibility of a backchannel conspiracy must not have seemed too far-fetched to Safire.

Another incident just prior to the presidential election in 1976 demonstrated the depth of Kissinger's antipathy to publicly flaying the Soviet Union over human rights. In one of their face-to-face meetings Kissinger had mentioned to Dobrynin that some Jewish visitors were harassed during a recent trip to the Soviet Union. By mutual consent their discussions were always private, but on October 29 Dobrynin read an *Associated Press* story stating that Kissinger had publicly criticized Moscow over the incident:

D: ...The Secretary of State Henry Kissinger today protested the harassment of Jews.

K: Total, absolute, outrageous!

---

[137] Kissinger Transcripts. U.S. Department of State; Kissinger, *Diplomacy*, 754.

D: This is what [State Department spokesman Robert] Funseth said.

K: Well, god damn these bastards. I said…

D: This is record.

K: I haven't seen the transcript. What I told him to say was if the question was asked was that our position on this issue was known.

D: But I have an AP ticker…

K: Let me first look at what was actually said will you?

D: All right.

K: I can't believe that Funseth said this.

D: This was on AP.

K: I don't believe he said that. It is inconceivable that he said this. Let me find out and I will call you back in five minutes.[138]

After receiving a transcript, Kissinger immediately called Dobrynin back:

K: Anatol, there was absolutely nothing said about a protest.

D: But…

K: Wait a minute, I am just telling you what the text says. It did not discuss the harassment of Jewish visitors. The answer is "the situation of Jews in the Soviet Union was discussed." Then it says can you be more specific. And the transcript says "I cannot be more specific." That is all

---

[138] Kissinger Transcripts. U.S. Department of State.

he said.   All he said was the situation of Jews   was discussed.

Then later…

> D: The whole implication is that it was a protest of the harassment of Jews.

> K: Did you read the whole text?

> D: No, I didn't.

> K: I think if you read the text…

> D: It is very clear…

> K: Look, I think if you read the whole transcript.

> D: You have never published our meetings and why was it necessary to do it today.[?][139]

Although Dobrynin thought Kissinger had violated a confidence by publicly discussing the specifics of one of their private meetings, the conversation between Funseth and the AP reporter was actually in the context of the 1976 presidential campaign. As Kissinger explained it, a reporter had asked, "Gov. Carter has expressed concern about what is going on about Soviet Jews. Has the US done anything on this?"[140] To which Funseth replied, "I cannot answer specifically but the Soviet Union is very much aware of our position on Soviet Jews."[141] The exchange had been in regard to the already much-publicized issue of Jewish emigration from the Soviet Union, not about the recent harassment of some Jewish visitors to the USSR which Kissinger and Dobrynin had discussed privately. "I regret it Anatol, I genuinely regret it," pleaded Kissinger.[142] Once Dobrynin had a proper understanding of the context of the

---

[139] Ibid.

[140] Ibid.

[141] Ibid.

[142] Ibid.

conversation, he calmed down considerably. As they had done so often before, Kissinger and Dobrynin had cleared up a major misunderstanding.

This entire episode was telling in that Kissinger displayed far more outrage at being accused of publicly criticizing the Soviet Union for human rights abuses than he ever showed for the actual abuses themselves. His belief in quiet diplomacy as the proper way to handle these matters would never allow him to embarrass Dobrynin or the Soviets in such a public way. Although morally questionable, this shared view of Kissinger and Dobrynin on the impropriety of publicly discussing a nation's internal affairs was one of the main reasons why their relationship worked so successfully over the years. While the succeeding Carter administration chose to openly stand on principle and make human rights one of the focal points of its foreign policy, Kissinger simply avoided discussing the issue publicly in favor of making progress in other areas.

What was the correct strategy? Through private diplomacy in the backchannel, Jewish emigration rose dramatically. When the issue surfaced in official channels, however, it triggered a strong reaction from the Soviet leadership and the numbers plummeted. From a high of 35,000 in 1973, emigration numbers dropped to 21,000 in 1974 and to a mere 13,000 in 1975.[143] Although the total rebounded to 50,000 in 1979 after President Carter promised to repeal *Jackson-Vanik*, in the 1980s virtually all emigration stopped.[144] Nevertheless, over thirty years from 1975-2005 approximately 1,000,000 Jews emigrated from the Soviet Union to Israel with another 573,000 arriving in the United States.[145]

Perhaps the most significant effect of *Jackson-Vanik* may have been the damage done to relaxing tensions. The period from 1975 to 1980 featured renewed confrontations between the United States and the Soviet Union around the world through various proxies. Kissinger was unsure if Soviet moves including increased military deliveries to Vietnam and arms to communist forces in Angola were signs of Soviet disillusionment with détente or part of a larger long-term strategy.[146] On the other hand, it is doubtful whether the economic benefits of increased trade and credits with the United States would have been significant enough to dissuade the

---

[143] Garthoff, *Détente and Confrontation*, 461.

[144] Garthoff, *Détente and Confrontation*, 1124; Gelman, 147.

[145] The White House, *Jackson-Vanik and Russia Fact Sheet*, 2005. Available at www.whitehouse.gov.

[146] Kissinger, *Years of Renewal*, 308.

Politburo from their course of action during the succeeding years anyway.[147]

The Helsinki Accords

In the summer of 1945 as the Second World War came to an end, the American, British, and Soviet allies met in Potsdam, Germany where Moscow received a tacit acceptance of its occupation of Eastern Europe.[148] During the Cold War the Soviets sought to ensure their security by maintaining communist regimes in the countries along their western border. After Moscow invaded Czechoslovakia in 1968 to halt anti-Soviet reforms by Alexander Dubcek's government, the Kremlin must have concluded that additional measures were necessary. According to Zubok, Brezhnev feared "'falling dominoes'" in Central Europe just as Lyndon Johnson had feared them in Southeast Asia.[149] Consequently, at Warsaw Pact meetings in October and December of 1969 the Soviets proposed a European Security Conference to be held the next year.[150]

Initially, Moscow hoped to exclude Washington from the meeting.[151] Kissinger speculated that the Soviets may have hoped to split the Western alliance and convince the Europeans to abandon NATO (the North Atlantic Treaty Alliance) in favor of some new security arrangement.[152] He considered this an utter fantasy: "No NATO country was waiting to substitute the declaratory bureaucratic paraphernalia of a European Security Conference for the military reality of NATO or the presence of American military forces on the Continent."[153] Since Washington's participation was a *sine qua non* for any security conference, the Nixon administration used it as another carrot of détente.[154] The United States made Soviet restraint in the developing world, Western access to Berlin, and mutual reduction of armed forces in Europe conditions for its participation.[155]

---

[147] Gelman, 151.

[148] Ulam, 141.

[149] Zubok, 207.

[150] Thornton, 30.

[151] Ibid., 30-31.

[152] Kissinger, *Diplomacy*, 758.

[153] Ibid.

[154] Ibid.

[155] Ibid., 759.

In addition to covering security and trade, the conference would also address human rights in part to prevent repeats of Soviet crackdowns on dissenters in East Germany (1953), Hungary (1956), and Czechoslovakia (1968).[156] However, during an address to the Soviet people during his first visit to Moscow in 1972 Nixon had said, "'We believe in the right of each nation to chart its own course, to choose its own system, to go its own way, without interference from other nations.'"[157] Reconciling the contradiction between this statement and upholding international human rights norms hampered détente throughout the rest of the decade.

Although many in the West viewed the Kremlin as a violator of human rights, the issue had to be considered in the context of Soviet history. The loss of twenty million people during the Second World War undoubtedly influenced the Soviet view that the right to life was the greatest human right of all. Therefore by preserving peace first and foremost, you protected human rights. For example, during his speech at the European Security Conference, Brezhnev remarked, "[W]e would like to stress most emphatically one of the inherent features of the foreign policy of the Soviet Union, of the Leninist policy of peace and friendship among nations – its humanism."[158] Gromyko perhaps framed the Soviet position most succinctly: "[O]nly if you are alive can you enjoy all the other rights – the right to work, to housing, education, medical service, emigration and so on."[159]

On March 15, 1973, just months prior to the opening of negotiations, Dobrynin inquired about the chance of the US withdrawing its support for a human rights commission. It is not clear if this referred to the inclusion of human rights at the European Security Conference itself or more probably to the creation of a group to monitor human rights compliance thereafter. What is certain is that Dobrynin disdained any notion of interfering in the Soviet Union's domestic policies, and Kissinger seemed only too happy to oblige:

---

[156] Kissinger, *Years of Renewal*, 639.

[157] John J. Maresca, *To Helsinki* (Durham, North Carolina: Duke University Press, 1985), 12.

[158] Leonid Brezhnev, "Speech at the Conference on Security and Cooperation in Europe Held in Helsinki," July 31, 1975, in *Peace, Détente, and Cooperation*, translated (New York: Consultants Bureau, 1981), 26.

[159] Andrei Gromyko, *Memoirs*, translated by Harold Shukman (New York: Doubleday, 1989), 293.

D: Have you by chance mention[ed] to your State Department about this Human Rights Commission?

K: I have talked to [US Ambassador to the Soviet Union Kenneth] Rush. I will have an answer for you within an hour. He was going to check.

D: Oh, check, yes. Okay. *Just to know whether he is checking or not on stopping all this nonsense.* [italics mine]

K: Right.[160]

A little over an hour later Kissinger called back:

K: On the Human Rights thing, we cancelled the instructions.

D: They cancelled?

K: Yes.

D: I think this is a very good idea and I will send a telegram to Gromyko right away.[161]

Despite Kissinger's efforts, however, the US government would eventually establish a commission to monitor compliance with Helsinki's human rights provisions.

In May, diplomats from thirty-three European countries, the United States, and Canada commenced negotiations in Geneva, Switzerland for the Conference on Security and Cooperation in Europe (CSCE). By the following year, negotiations had advanced sufficiently to consider holding a summit to sign the conference's concluding document.[162] However, in a conversation with Dobrynin on July 12, 1974, Kissinger asked for a little help on "basket III" – human rights, and downplayed the notion of holding a formal summit meeting:

---

[160] [March 1973. Box #27.]

[161] Ibid.

[162] Kissinger, *Years of Renewal*, 641.

K: ...I want to tell you what we have done on the European Security Conference, because I think we have got it in a very positive direction now, if you cooperate a little bit on Basket III.

D: Well, do you have any concrete suggestions? This is important.

K: I think we have broken the back on the Summit idea.

D: Already.

K: I think we are well on the way. But don't go around saying this.

D: No. no, no.

K: No, you won't, but sometimes your people in the lower regions are not as subtle as you are.

D: On this only Gromyko and myself are looking, otherwise he will keep this close to his heart. It is a project he likes very much.[163]

The last thing Dobrynin or Kissinger wanted was to have a summit-level meeting calling attention to human rights – an issue they both preferred to handle privately. In addition, Kissinger probably opposed a summit for domestic political reasons. In May, 1975 as the summit approached, he warned President Ford that Senator Jackson and others would claim the conference was a fraud and a total sellout of Eastern Europe.[164] This would undoubtedly agitate Eastern European immigrants, as well as those from the Baltic nations of Latvia, Lithuania, and Estonia which could not participate because they had been incorporated into the Union of Soviet Socialist Republics.[165] Ford admitted that a sampling of his mail from Eastern European émigrés showed 558 opposed to only 32 in favor of the

---

[163] [January 1974-August 1974. Box #28.]
[164] Kissinger, *Years of Renewal*, 645.
[165] Ibid.

Helsinki Accounds.[166] Nevertheless, when the conference was held Kissinger believed Ford felt compelled to attend in order to maintain momentum on détente and avoid returning to a state of "Cold War."[167]

While Ford sought to preserve détente, Aleksandr Solzhenitsyn endeavored to destroy it. On June 30, George Meany and the AFL-CIO invited the Soviet exile to speak at a Washington dinner.[168] Kissinger alleged that Solzhenitsyn, a Nobel Prize winner for *The Gulag Archipelago* (a massive expose of the Soviet slave labor camps), had been chosen to speak by the staunchly anti-communist Meany in order to provide ammunition to opponents of the European Security Conference which was scheduled for the following month.[169] Speaking of the impending Helsinki *Final Act*, Solzhenitsyn asked:

> What sort of an agreement would this be? The proposed agreement is the funeral of eastern Europe. It means that western Europe would finally, once and for all, sign away eastern Europe, stating that it is perfectly willing to see eastern Europe be crushed and overwhelmed once and for all, but please don't bother us.[170]

Then a few days later controversy exploded when Ford had an opportunity to meet with Solzhenitsyn. Kissinger, who professed a deep personal admiration for the Soviet writer, claimed that the meeting never took place due to a scheduling conflict, but also argued that it would have been a mistake for reasons of policy as well.[171] Ford noted that both Kissinger and Deputy National Security Advisor Brent Scowcroft had recommended against a meeting.[172] Kissinger's reasoning was that since White House requests had contributed to Solzhenitsyn's recent release, if Ford met with him it could appear as gloating, particularly just prior to meeting Brezhnev

---

[166] Ford, 301.

[167] Kissinger, *Years of Renewal*, 645.

[168] Ibid., 649.

[169] Ibid.

[170] Aleksandr Solzhenitsyn, "America: You Must Think About the World," June 30, 1975, in *Détente – Prospects for Democracy and Dictatorship* (New Brunswick, New Jersey: Transaction Books, 1976), 31.

[171] Kissinger, *Years of Renewal*, 649, 650.

[172] Ford, 298.

in Helsinki.[173]   Jackson, *The Wall Street Journal*, *The New York Times*, and many others vociferously disagreed.[174]

On July 30 and August 1, 1975, representatives of thirty-five countries met in Helsinki to sign the *Final Act* of the Conference on Security and Cooperation in Europe (CSCE).[175] Also known as the *Helsinki Accords*, the CSCE's *Final Act* was intended to improve East-West relations on multiple levels. Basket I dealt with security, which for the Soviets chiefly meant Western acceptance of the communist regimes established in Eastern Europe after the Second World War. Basket II covered economics, science, technology, and the environment.[176] The most controversial issue – human rights – was reserved for basket III. The act obligated countries to:

> ...promote and encourage the effective exercise of civil, political, economic, social, cultural and other rights and freedoms all of which derive from the inherent dignity of the human person...[177]

Finally, a fourth basket outlined procedures to follow up on the first three.[178]

Dobrynin admitted that for the Soviet Union basket III was merely a formality. He claimed that the prime interests of his government were security and trade and that Moscow "did all it could to diminish the significance of the third basket, for it still believed humanitarian issues to be domestic matters."[179] When Gromyko reported on the final document to the Politburo, "they were stunned."[180] Chairman of the Supreme Soviet Nikolai Podgorny, Chief Ideologist Mikhail Suslov, Prime Minister Alexei Kosygin, and KGB leader Yuri Andropov were among those most opposed to the human rights provisions, but Brezhnev clamored for the prestige he would garner back home from signing an international

---

[173] Kissinger, *Years of Renewal*, 651.

[174] Ibid.

[175] Dobrynin, *In Confidence*, 350.

[176] Vogelgesang, 222.

[177] Conference on Security and Cooperation in Europe, *Final Act*, 1 August 1975.

[178] Stevenson, 172.

[179] Dobrynin, *In Confidence*, 350.

[180] Ibid., 351.

agreement ratifying the post-WWII borders of Europe.[181] Gromyko alleviated the Politburo's fears when he explained, "We are masters in our own house," suggesting that the Soviet leadership retained the right to determine what amounted to interference in its internal affairs.[182]

While basket III caused controversy in the Soviet Union, elsewhere the security provisions of basket I provoked outrage. Brezhnev referred to these provisions as "a necessary summing up of the political results of World War II."[183] The Soviet effort to legitimize the boundaries of Eastern Europe dated back to the 1950s.[184] For Moscow, permanent boundaries not only signified security, but also the acceptance of communism across half a continent.[185] Keith L. Nelson called the Helsinki conference "an East-West compromise in the best sense of the word."[186] However, David Pryce-Jones charged that it had "confirmed the Soviet Union in its invasion and occupation of Eastern and Central Europe."[187] He likened it to the 1938 Munich Agreement between Britain and Nazi Germany which Hitler violated shortly thereafter, prompting World War II: "In effect, the Soviet Union had won that stage of the Cold War, and was poised to move to complete supremacy over the remaining European democracies."[188] East Germany's Erich Honecker believed that his nation had finally achieved legitimacy, and therefore any reunification with West Germany "could now only be on Soviet terms."[189] Similarly, Poland's General Wojciech Jaruzelski was convinced that the Communist bloc had never been stronger.[190]

Kissinger viewed Western acknowledgement of the permanency of Europe's borders as a harmless token thrown to the Soviets in order to enhance their sense of security. He argued that the American delegation

---

[181] Ibid.

[182] Ibid.

[183] Leonid Brezhnev, "Speech at the Conference on Security and Cooperation in Europe Held in Helsinki," July 31, 1975, in *Peace, Détente, and Cooperation*, translated (New York: Consultants Bureau, 1981), 22.

[184] Melvin Leffler, *For the Soul of Mankind – The United States, The Soviet Union, and the Cold War* (New York: Hill and Wang, 2007), 234.

[185] Ibid., 235.

[186] Nelson, 147.

[187] David Pryce-Jones, *The Strange Death of the Soviet Empire* (New York: Metropolitan Books, 1995), 74.

[188] Ibid.

[189] Ibid.

[190] Ibid.

had only conceded that borders could not be changed by force, merely echoing the UN Charter.[191] Not only did this repudiate the Brezhnev Doctrine (justifying Soviet military action in order to preserve socialist unity), Kissinger believed it helped lead to eventual German reunification in 1990.[192]

Dissidents behind the Iron Curtain were not as patient as Kissinger. For them the *Final Act* was much more than a piece of paper. It signified that human rights had become a part of international law.[193] Many viewed it as either a tool for reform in the Soviet Union and Eastern Europe or at least a means of escape.[194] On April 12, 1976, eleven Soviet dissidents including Yuri Orlov, Anatoly Sharansky, Ludmilla Alexeeva, and Elena Bonner founded a Moscow "Helsinki Watch" group to monitor compliance with the accords and report violations.[195] Orlov explained that although they could not directly petition their own government, the Helsinki *Final Act* would allow them to reach the Soviets "'through the governments of other countries.'"[196] Additional monitoring groups quickly appeared in nearly all of the communist nations.[197] In theory at least, the means were in place to hold all thirty-five signatories accountable for human rights.[198]

However, the years following the signing of the *Helsinki Accords* were marked by both poor follow-up and compliance. A provision in the *Final Act* prohibiting interference in a country's internal affairs proved problematic.[199] Furthermore, because the accords emboldened dissenters to go public, this led to more intense persecution.[200] The seventy-five open members of monitoring groups in Armenia, Georgia, Lithuania, and other countries in addition to Russia and Ukraine either ended up in prison, work camps, psychiatric hospitals, or exile.[201] The Moscow

---

[191] Kissinger, *Diplomacy*, 759.

[192] Kissinger, *Years of Renewal*, 644, 648.

[193] Ibid., 648.

[194] Vogelgesang, 223.

[195] Anatoly Sharansky with Ron Dermer, *The Case for Democracy – The Power of Freedom to overcome Tyranny and Terror* (New York: Public Affairs, 2004), 129, 130.

[196] Paul Gordon Lauren, *The Evolution of International Human Rights* (Philadelphia: University of Pennsylvania Press, 2003), 260.

[197] Vogelgesang, 223.

[198] Ibid.

[199] Ibid.

[200] Johnson, 680.

[201] Edwards, 635.

Helsinki Watch group was out of business by 1982, and other monitoring groups like the Working Commission to Investigate the Abuse of Psychiatry for Political Purposes and the Christian Committee to Defend Believers Rights in the USSR faced persecution.[202] In 1983, the Soviet Union left the World Psychiatry Association (WPA) just prior to a final judgment on its continued membership.[203] The USSR's expulsion from the WPA was probably imminent because the Soviet state had viewed political opponents as mentally ill ever since Lenin.[204] Furthermore, Soviet psychiatric hospitals were under the Ministry of the Interior, not Health, and were run like prisons by military officers.[205]

Numerous reports of the United States Commission on Security and Cooperation in Europe (US CSCE or US Helsinki Watch) noted that many countries had not met the human rights standards agreed to at Helsinki.[206] For example, in 1985 the commission reported:

> Ten years after Helsinki, the Helsinki groups that formed in the USSR have virtually disbanded, with more than fifty Helsinki monitors presently in prison or exile. In Czechoslovakia, Charter 77 signatories and their families continue to be persecuted...The Polish Helsinki Committee that flourished openly during the days when Solidarity was legal has been forced underground.[207]

Bulgaria, Czechoslovakia, East Germany, Hungary, Poland, Romania, Turkey, the USSR and Yugoslavia were listed as the nine worst violators of freedom of speech, the press, movement, association, religion, and freedom from political imprisonment and torture.[208] The lack of compliance illustrated the great chasm between the American and Soviet conceptions of human rights and détente. Although Kissinger and Dobrynin understood this better than anyone else, as the issue became

---

[202] Ibid.

[203] Ibid.

[204] Johnson, 680.

[205] Ibid., 680, 681.

[206] Vogelgesang, 230.

[207] The United States Helsinki Watch Committee, *The Years Later: Violations of the Helsinki Accords* (New York and Washington, D.C., 1985), ii.

[208] Ibid., v.

public there was less they could do in the backchannel to manage its effects on relaxing tensions.

A Few "Hardship Cases"

In addition to the broader topics of Jewish emigration and international human rights, Kissinger and Dobrynin handled numerous cases involving individual Soviet and American citizens. Kissinger described "a list of hardship cases" which the White House occasionally provided to the Kremlin involving people who had been denied exit visas, separated from their families, or imprisoned – often for political reasons.[209] He claimed that many of the requests were successful, including 550 out of 800 in 1973.[210]

For example, on June 6, 1972, Kissinger inquired about a Soviet citizen who was married to an American. The conversation did not emphasize humanitarian interests or principles, but simply addressed the case in terms of political pressure and its potential effects upon detente:

> K: Now let me raise an issue with you. It has to do with Shapiro. We are not taking an official position. We're being deluged with phone calls from senators and Senator Jackson called yesterday and he was going to make a public statement and I urged him to keep quiet and I just wanted to express the view that if this thing could be diffused. I don't know a damn thing about it. I don't know what the fellow did. I think he's the fellow who married this American girl.

> D: But the question was he was subject to the military draft. He evaded it and then he met this American girl and married. So...

> K: He's not American. We can't get into the Soviet side of it. It's merely a case where we are under a lot of pressure. This is not going to be made a matter of record and we will never even acknowledge that I have even talked to you about it.

---

[209] Kissinger, *Diplomacy*, 753; Kissinger, *White House Years*, 1271.
[210] Kissinger, *White House Years*, 1271.

D: The difficulty is he evaded the military draft. Well, I will mention to my people about what you mentioned.

K: Just mention really we are under terrific Senatorial pressure and we are not making an official reference to it.[211]

While Dobrynin could not guarantee anything, he was willing to take the Shapiro case to his superiors because he understood the political pressure Kissinger was facing. Likewise, Kissinger acknowledged that this was not an ordinary case of a citizen seeking to emigrate. Shapiro had violated Soviet law, thereby complicating the situation further.

Two months later on August 2, Kissinger returned the favor. The Chairman of the Evangelical Baptist Church of the Soviet Union, Alexi Eychkov, was visiting the United States and had requested to meet with President Nixon. When Dobrynin expressed his concerns, Kissinger did not hesitate:

K: ...we have a request here that the Chairman of the Evangelical Baptist Church of the Soviet Union.

D: What's his name?

K: Schweitkof (sp.?)

D: He is the Chairman of the Baptist Church?

K: In the Soviet Union. The General Secretary of the Church, Alexi Eychkov and two others want to call on the President. They are traveling in this country and the reason for doing it is because the President attended his church in Moscow. Now this is of course an informal request. Can you give me an...

D: When will it be?

K: I think tomorrow or the day after.

---

[211] [May 1972–June 1972. Box #27.]

D: Tomorrow. I don't think it is in general a good idea.
That's my impression.

K: OK, well I'll stop it. It's easy to stop. I see no reason to
do it to tell you the truth.

D: Yeh, I think it is not a good idea.

K: No, we just won't do it.[212]

What did Eychkov want to say to the President? Was it simply a friendly visit or did he seek to lodge a complaint against the Soviet government – perhaps relating to the denial of exit visas to Soviet Jews or about the issue of religious freedom in the Soviet Union? Whatever the reason may have been, Dobrynin was opposed to it and that was all that mattered to Kissinger.

A much more prominent case involved a Lithuanian sailor named Simas Kudirka. In November, 1970, Kudirka attempted to defect from the Soviet Union by boarding a US Coast Guard vessel off of Massachusetts.[213] Although he sought asylum, the American crew permitted Soviet sailors to forcibly retrieve the would-be defector.[214] The Lithuanian was then promptly placed in prison where he had remained for four years.

The United States government later discovered that Kudirka's mother had been born in the United States, suggesting the possibility of American citizenship. On August 14, 1974, President Ford met with Kissinger and Dobrynin in the Oval Office.[215] Calling it "a personal favor," Ford requested that the Soviets release Kudirka.[216] Dobrynin said he would pass it along to his government.[217] Over the next two weeks Ford and Brezhnev negotiated Kudirka's release and later his emigration to the United States.[218] On August 29, Kissinger thanked his counterpart for his assistance:

---

[212] [July 1972–September 1972. Box #27.]

[213] Kissinger, *White House Years*, 795.

[214] Ibid.

[215] Ford, 138.

[216] Ibid., 138, 139.

[217] Ibid., 139.

[218] Kissinger, *White House Years*, 795, 796.

K: I called you because of the Kidirka [sic] case. We have been informed that he [has] been released and the President [wanted] to express his appreciation but he didn't know how to do it. - - in a way that wouldn't be difficult for you.

D: No, no. Let me make it - - I will give you tomorrow something and we can discuss this then. No appreciation is necessary. We will talk tomorrow about it. I am expecting a message from Brezhnev.

K: I will tell you what he [Ford] said….they should not make a big fuss over it but he wants them to know this was a result of peaceful relations…and this is an example of what can be done without pressure but in a ….relationship.

D: I understand. I understand.

K: He is going to tell some people on the Hill about this…[219]

Once again, quiet diplomacy had come through, and the White House would make sure that Congress knew about it.

The Soviets often denied exit visas for security reasons. These claims could seem arbitrary and certainly aroused suspicions in the US, but Moscow's concerns about a Russian woman married to an American professor may have been quite genuine. Dobrynin's candid statements from January 21, 1975, suggested that the woman may have been involved with Soviet agents:

K: There is a professor [name expunged]

D: A difficult case.

K: It is. Can you tell me personally what the problem is. He is married to a Russian…

[219] Kissinger Transcripts. U.S. Department of State.

D: Yes. This is the problem. Only yesterday I received some information on this and it is a difficult case. The [girl] is involved in a certain kind of thing dealing with our security. Don't mention this please.

K: No, but it will affect my action on this. He [the American professor] has been decent in the manner in which he is pushing it.

D: I know. There was some White House-State Department influence.

K: I have stayed out of it up to now.

D: One of your assistants mentioned it to me and I checked it with Moscow two weeks ago: Just yesterday I received a telegram.

K: I don't know the [situation?] at all.

D: It is nothing for herself as such but she was involved in - - nothing specifically about her and I know nothing really. But this is why I am prepared to give you an immediate answer. Only yesterday I received information telling me it is a difficult case. [The Kremlin?] did note your views - - in any case they know about the State Department views. I am being honest with you by telling you I received this information just yesterday.

K: You know the problems on humanity grounds. It is a deserving case. I don't know the security situation.

D: It is in Moscow. She worked with some of our agenst [sic] - - I should not say this.

K: I understand.

D: That is why they don't want to let her go. This is very personal information I am giving to you. She is not a professor really and she is not a brilliant girl at all but she knows something because of the character of her record. While in Moscow I will mention it again to Gromyko.[220]

Even in a case such as this where Dobrynin doubted that his government would be able to grant Kissinger's request, he felt confident enough about the interpersonal relationship to disclose classified information, perhaps even against his better judgment.

Finally, when an American received a death sentence in Angola, a Soviet ally, Kissinger did not hesitate to call Dobrynin among others. Although the United States had supported a rival faction during the Angolan Civil War and did not recognize the new Marxist regime, on June 29, 1976, Kissinger inquired if Dobrynin could intervene:

> K: ...Now Anatol, I am calling you about this death sentence to the American in Angola. I know it isn't a question of the Soviet Union having anything to do with it directly, but we would appreciate it very much since we have no diplomatic relations [with Angola] if our concern could be conveyed to the Angolan government or if you could use your influence on a personal basis. I think you know what will happen here if this is carried out...

> D: How many Americans - - one or two?

> K: One...

Then later...

> D: Well I will send a telegram that you mentioned it...

> K: That is right.

> D: No specific obligations, but at the same time human concern.

---

220 Ibid.

K: O.K. Anatol, thank you very much.[221]

Although Kissinger claimed that he was acting for humanitarian reasons, he also intimated that if the American was executed by a Soviet ally, it would further turn Congressional and public opinion against détente.

The telephone transcripts showed that Kissinger and Dobrynin understood the domestic political pressure each faced as human rights became an increasingly salient issue in US-Soviet relations. The transcripts also revealed that for the Soviets human rights was a domestic affair and therefore out-of-bounds in international diplomacy. As Dobrynin put it in one telephone conversation with Kissinger regarding the European Security Conference, the inclusion of human rights was "nonsense." This sentiment was further demonstrated by the fact that whenever Moscow was accused of transgressing human rights norms, its response was not to charge Washington with hypocrisy and cite discrimination against African-Americans, women, or the poor in the United States. Rather, the Kremlin's typical answer amounted to: "It's none of your damn business."

In the short run, the injection of human rights into détente hurt many of the people it was meant to protect and strained US-Soviet relations. Jewish emigration slowed to a trickle after *Jackson-Vanik*. The *Helsinki Accords* emboldened many dissidents, but brought increased repression as a result. However, such measures helped to establish a legal and institutional basis for human rights advocates in the East and West to mount a successful defense of individual freedoms. An argument could be made that this not only had a positive effect for the state of human rights, but also contributed to delegitimizing totalitarian regimes in the Soviet Union and Eastern bloc and helped lead to the end of the Cold War. Although Kissinger and Dobrynin had success with their private approach, in the long run publicly standing on principle was the right thing to do for reasons of both humanity and policy.

---

221 Ibid.

Chapter 4

Foreign Interventions: Preserving Stability or National Liberation?

"...I believe détente mitigated the succession of crises that differences in ideology and geopolitical interest had made nearly inevitable; and I believe we enhanced the national interest in the process."
-Henry Kissinger[1]

"...the crisis [the October 1973 Arab-Israeli/Yom Kippur War] demonstrated that tension could be localized and prevented from disrupting relations between Washington and Moscow. This was the first serious international conflict under the conditions of détente, which was strongly affected by it."
-Anatoly Dobrynin[2]

During the Cold War the United States and the Soviet Union never fought each other directly on the battlefield. However, they did battle indirectly via proxies in Asia, Africa, and Latin America, with the international competition reaching a crescendo in the 1970s. These interventions included massive arms sales around the world totaling billions of dollars.[3] When considered alongside cases of direct involvement by one or the other superpower as with the Americans in Vietnam or the Soviets in Afghanistan, the global extent of the ideological struggle at times resembled a kind of world war. British historian Paul Johnson likened the period to that just preceding World War II: "The extension of the Cold War, during the Seventies, to virtually every part of the globe, gave the decade the air of chronic insecurity so characteristic of the Thirties – the same syndrome of unemployment, economic decay, armaments and aggression."[4] However, the deterrent effects of the atomic age prevented a head-to-head hot war which could have escalated into nuclear Armageddon.

---

[1] Henry Kissinger, *Years of Upheaval* (New York: Simon & Schuster, 1982), 600.

[2] Anatoly Dobrynin, *In Confidence – Moscow's Ambassador to America's Six Cold War Presidents* (New York: Times Books, 1995), 292.

[3] Paul Johnson, *Modern Times – The World from the Twenties to the Nineties* (New York: HarperCollins Publishers, 1991), 685.

[4] Ibid.

Although the Cold War never turned hot, the conflicting views of relaxing tensions nevertheless extended into the military sphere. The Americans had an all-encompassing conception of détente and objected when the Soviets intervened in the national liberation movements of former European colonies in the developing world. The US viewed this as destabilizing and not in the spirit of relaxing tensions. However, the Soviets saw no contradiction between conducting *razryadka* with the Americans while also assisting young nations in their efforts to achieve true political and economic independence from the West. For the USSR, one had nothing to do with the other.

Foreign interventions posed the gravest challenge to détente and the Kissinger-Dobrynin relationship. Due to the possibility of direct conflict and even war, conversations dealing with the US-Soviet global competition dominated the telephone conversation transcripts. The telcons showed that even during détente, Moscow's actions and Washington's reactions were often driven by ideology.

Foreign Interventions and Détente

Foreign interventions in the developing world were more than mere efforts to protect security and economic interests. Marxist-Leninist ideology played a crucial role in Soviet actions, although it is unclear if the ideological concept of "wars of liberation" from capitalist domination started with Lenin, Khrushchev, or Brezhnev. Meanwhile, the Americans often reacted to Soviet actions out of an ideological belief in the inherent benefits of democracy and free market capitalism to nations around the world.

Writing in the wake of the Soviet invasion of Afghanistan, author, historian, and former army lieutenant colonel F. Charles Parker claimed that the nations of the "Third World" remained part of a Soviet strategy "fundamentally unchanged since 1920."[5] Furthermore, Parker argued that the Soviet Union had consistently sought "to create tensions and divisions in the non-Communist world, including both the advanced capitalist nations and the backward areas of the Third World, in order to achieve strategic gains for the Soviet state," and "Soviet domination of the world."[6] According to this line of reasoning, when Vladimir Lenin (r. 1917-1924) realized that the instability brought on by World War I had

---

[5] F. Charles Parker, "The Third World in Soviet Strategy, 1945-1980," *Asian Affairs* Vol.7, No. 6 (Jul. – Aug., 1980), 341.

[6] Ibid.

dissipated and his predicted workers' revolutions in the West were not imminent, he proclaimed at the Second Congress of the Communist International in July, 1920, that Soviet foreign policy should seek to exploit differences among non-communist nations.[7] By depriving Europe and America of colonies in the developing world, the Soviets would ensure that the capitalists had less material wealth with which to "bribe" their workers into accepting the class-based status quo.[8] According to Parker, every Soviet leader since the revolution claimed to be both a Leninist and a supporter of the same foreign policy objectives.[9]

More recently, Volkogonov asserted that what became known as the Brezhnev Doctrine in the West actually had a much older pedigree and was in fact "Leninist-Stalinist-Cominternist in origin."[10] He called the 1968 Soviet intervention in Czechoslovakia "a warning to other satellites that their sovereignty was secondary to their 'international duty'" as part of the global socialist movement.[11] Volkogonov implied that similar reasoning led to the 1979 invasion of Afghanistan.[12]

Adam Ulam argued that although there had been "precedents" under Lenin, the ideological concept of "'wars of liberation'" from capitalist domination actually emerged under Nikita Khrushchev (r. 1953-1964).[13] William Tompson agreed, stating that as long as a newly independent nation was anti-imperialist in its orientation, Khrushchev offered his support and thereby pre-empted indigenous communist parties.[14] According to Christopher Andrew and former KGB official Vasili Mitrokhin, Khrushchev became convinced by the decline of European colonial empires after World War II "to revive the Leninist dream" of world socialism.[15] Furthermore, Khrushchev believed that the

---

[7] Ibid., 342, 343.

[8] Ibid., 344.

[9] Ibid., 343.

[10] Dmitri Volkogonov, *Autopsy for an Empire – The Seven Leaders Who Build the Soviet Regime*, trans. Harold Shukman (New York: The Free Press, 1998), 292.

[11] Ibid.

[12] Ibid., 283.

[13] Adam B. Ulam, *Dangerous Relations – The Soviet Union in World Politics* (New York: Oxford University Press, 1983), 56.

[14] William Tompson, *The Soviet Union under Brezhnev* (Edinburgh: Pearson Education Ltd., 2003), 10.

[15] Christopher Andrew and Vasili Mitrokhin, *The World Was Going Our Way – The KGB and the Battle for the Third World* (New York: Basic Books, 2005), 1, 5.

Soviet success with rapid industrialization in the 1930s could be replicated in developing countries across the globe.[16]

Several scholars traced Soviet involvement in the developing world to the era of Leonid Brezhnev (r. 1964-1982). Garthoff wrote, "Detente and peaceful coexistence with the United States did not...mean any lessening of the global 'class struggle' or of Soviet support for progressive historical change."[17] He noted that Moscow made this point at the Twenty-fourth Party Congress in 1971 when presenting its conception of detente.[18] The Soviet leadership voiced similar sentiments at summit meetings with the US in 1972 and 1973.[19] Meanwhile, Daniels claimed that under Brezhnev there was "a vigorous political offensive," as Moscow sought to draw "one developing country after another away from dependence on the capitalists and making them allies of the socialist camp."[20] Although he believed that the strategy was "probably more opportunistic than premeditated," it nevertheless resulted in "America's reversion to the worst Cold War fears."[21] Likewise, Pryce-Jones argued that in Asia "'proletarian dictatorships'" emerged in Vietnam, Laos, and Cambodia.[22] In Africa, "a historical process of gaining independence from the colonial powers was reversed," and the Congo, Benin, Ethiopia, Mozambique, and Angola became "Soviet clients."[23] Finally, Central America became "destabilized" after the Soviet-supported Sandinistas took control of Nicaragua.[24] He added that while other empires made "profit-and-loss calculations" leading to decolonization, communism renewed the imperial drive through its fundamental doctrine of "'world revolution.'"[25]

Zubok claimed that "the majority of the post-Khrushchev leadership shared the ideological (revolutionary) component of the

---

[16] Ibid., 5.

[17] Raymond L. Garthoff, *Détente and Confrontation – American Soviet Relations from Nixon to Reagan* (Washington, D.C.: The Brookings Institution, 1985), 530.

[18] Ibid.

[19] Ibid.

[20] Robert V. Daniels, *The End of the Communist Revolution* (New York: Routledge, 1993), 160.

[21] Ibid.

[22] David Pryce-Jones, *The Strange Death of the Soviet Empire* (New York: Metropolitan Books, 1995), 20.

[23] Ibid.

[24] Ibid.

[25] Ibid., 63.

international paradigm."[26] However, he suggested that rather than being pure ideologues, the détente-era generation of Soviet leaders were "prisoners of ideology," who knew of no other way and therefore were unable to change course.[27] Leffler was blunter. He argued that Brezhnev "killed détente with the United States, the policy he had helped to launch a decade before," by invading Afghanistan in 1979.[28] He added that Brezhnev "shamelessly defended Soviet actions" and claimed that Moscow was merely "answering the request of the Afghan government" for protection.[29]

Georgi I. Mirski, a chief research fellow at the Institute of World Economy and International Relations in Moscow, Russian Academy of Sciences, argued that détente ended "mainly, although not exclusively, because of developments in the third world."[30] Wanting to assert their role as the leaders of international communism, the Soviets felt compelled to assist national liberation movements before the Chinese took action.[31] Furthermore, with nuclear parity and the division of Europe into eastern and western halves, the US-Soviet competition was at a relative standstill.[32] The nations of Asia, Africa, and Latin America represented the only remaining potential battlefields. Consequently, Mirski concluded: "It was in the shifting sands of the third world, a battlefield of maneuver warfare, that new and unforeseen collisions between the superpowers could be expected, and they did not take long to materialize."[33]

Other scholars argued that both superpowers took actions in the developing world for ideological reasons. Edward J. Brennan, Ireland's ambassador to Moscow from 1974-1980, stated that the United States and the Soviet Union were "by history and national character...prone to

---

[26] Vladislav Zubok, *A Failed Empire – The Soviet Union in the Cold War from Stalin to Gorbachev* (Chapel Hill: University of North Carolina Press, 2007), 196.

[27] Ibid.

[28] Melvin Leffler, *For the Soul of Mankind – The United States, the Soviet Union, and the Cold War* (New York: Hill and Wang, 2007), 334.

[29] Ibid., 335.

[30] Georgi I. Mirski, "Soviet-American Relations in the Third World," in *Turning Points in Ending the Cold War*, ed. Kiron K. Skinner (Stanford, California: Hoover Institution Press, 2008), 162.

[31] Ibid., 159.

[32] Ibid., 162.

[33] Ibid.

ideology in the conduct of their foreign relations."[34] For example, Thomas Jefferson believed that the United States would serve as a "'standing monument and example for the aim and emulation by the rest of the world.'"[35] Brennan also pointed to the ideological tenor of American foreign policy under President Ronald Reagan, who in a 1982 address before the British Parliament launched a "'crusade for freedom'" which would "'leave Marxism-Leninism on the ash-heap of history.'"[36] Likewise, Brennan claimed that two ideological principles drove Soviet foreign policy, specifically proletarian internationalism and peaceful coexistence of states with different social systems.[37] The first referred to "the historic mission of the working class to establish socialism on a world scale," while the second applied exclusively to relations between *states*, with the international *class* struggle continuing.[38]

Similarly, Nelson claimed that "neither party to détente had promised to stop 'assisting' history or trying to head off what it considered to be unnatural developments in the Third World."[39] He suggested that during the 1970s decolonization spread to nations which were utterly unprepared for it, causing many countries to be thrown "into anarchic independence."[40] Nelson argued that the Soviet Union simply took advantage and "project[ed] itself into other countries' business" just as the US had often done.[41]

According to some, the Soviets and Americans felt compelled by domestic politics to spread their respective ideologies. James G. Richter argued that the superpowers "relied heavily on universalistic ideas to create a national identity."[42] He asserted that they "justified their foreign policies not only as a means to protect the national interest but also to protect and even propagate the way of life (whether Soviet-style socialism

---

[34] Edward J. Brennan, "East-West Relations: the Role of Ideology," *Irish Studies in International Affairs* Vol. 2, No. 1 (1985), 51.

[35] Ibid., 63.

[36] Ibid., 54, 57.

[37] Ibid., 61.

[38] Ibid., 64, 71, 72.

[39] Keith L. Nelson, *The Making of Détente – Soviet-American Relations in the Shadow of Vietnam* (Baltimore: The Johns Hopkins University Press, 1995), 148.

[40] Ibid.

[41] Ibid., 148, 149.

[42] James G. Richter, "Perpetuating the Cold War: Domestic Sources of International Patterns of Behavior," *Political Science Quarterly* Vol. 107, No. 2 (Summer, 1992), 275-276.

or liberal democracy) these ideas would prescribe."[43] These ideas or "myths" became part of each country's domestic politics and were "difficult to dislodge," he added.[44] Likewise, Odd Arne Westad wrote that Washington and Moscow "were driven to intervene in the Third World by the ideologies inherent in their politics."[45] Furthermore, he claimed that the United States and the Soviet Union "needed to change the world" to demonstrate "the universal applicability of their ideologies."[46]

Finally, John Lewis Gaddis asserted that "ideology often *determined* [italics in original] the behavior of Marxist-Leninist regimes: it was not simply a justification for actions already decided upon."[47] Consequently, the United States had to choose between upholding its own ideological principles – including the right to self-determination – and preserving its economic and security interests.[48] In no case was this paradox more evident than with the American intervention in Vietnam – something Gaddis called "the single greatest error the United States made in fighting the Cold War."[49]

Vietnam

The roots of the Vietnam War lay in the global movement towards colonial independence after World War II. In September, 1945, Ho Chi Minh declared Vietnamese independence from France, even quoting from the American *Declaration of Independence*.[50] Ho had worked with the American Office of Strategic Services – predecessor to the Central Intelligence Agency – during the war. However, on February 14, 1950, he met in Moscow with Mao Zedong and Joseph Stalin to request assistance in expelling the French.[51] Stalin may have preferred to avoid providing direct assistance so as to not hurt the electoral chances of the French communists in Paris, and instead directed Mao to aid Ho's forces in

---

[43] Ibid., 276.

[44] Ibid., 273.

[45] Odd Arne Westad, *The Global Cold War – Third World Interventions and the Making of Our Times* (New York: Cambridge University Press, 2007), 4.

[46] Ibid.

[47] John Lewis Gaddis, *We Now Know – Rethinking Cold War History* (New York: Oxford University Press, 1997), 290.

[48] Ibid., 152, 157.

[49] Ibid., 189.

[50] John Lewis Gaddis, *The Cold War – A New History* (New York: The Penguin Press, 2005), 58.

[51] Michael Lind, *Vietnam – The Necessary War* (New York: The Free Press, 1999), 1, 3.

Southeast Asia.[52] That year Beijing recognized the Democratic Republic of Vietnam and began sending supplies.[53] Mao later sent advisers to create Chinese-style reeducation camps as well.[54] Ho also adopted Mao's tactics of terror including executions of land owners, intellectuals, and other "class enemies."[55]

As the French attempted to maintain their empire, they sought support first from the British and then the Americans.[56] Nevertheless, France was defeated in 1954 at Dien Bien Phu with Indochina being divided into the three states of Vietnam, Laos, and Cambodia.[57] Vietnam itself was split into a communist north and a non-communist south along the seventeenth parallel.[58]

Depending on one's point of view, the US began supporting South Vietnam as either a bulwark against communism or in order to establish a "satellite regime"[59] in the region. Many Americans saw communism as an aggressive force opposed to democracy, human rights, and free markets, with the last of these being particularly concerning for the US as it worked to rebuild Japan after World War II.[60] Furthermore, America's economically devastated British allies needed access to rubber and tin from their nearby Malayan colony.[61] If communism triumphed in Vietnam, many feared that other Southeast Asian countries would fall into line "like dominoes," thus threatening US and Western interests. It was this "domino theory" which resulted in American military involvement, particularly after 1965. Years of fighting abroad and turmoil at home ensued for the United States. When the Americans finally left in 1973,

---

[52] Ibid., 8.

[53] James M. Morris, *America's Armed Forces – A History* (Englewood Cliffs, New Jersey: Prentice Hall, 1991), 335.

[54] Jean-Louis Margolin, "Vietnam and Laos: The Impasse of War Communism," trans. Jonathan Murphy and Mark Kramer in *The Black Book of Communism*, ed. Stephane Courtois, et al. (Cambridge, Massachusetts: Harvard University Press, 1999), 568.

[55] Lind, 10, 11.

[56] Eric Hobsbawm, *The Age of Extremes – A History of the World, 1914-1991* (New York: Pantheon Books, 1994), 217.

[57] Thomas C. Reed, *At the Abyss – An Insider's History of the Cold War* (New York: Ballantine Books, 2004), 144.

[58] Lind, 10.

[59] Hobsbawm, 217.

[60] John Whiteclay Chambers II, ed. *The Oxford Companion to American Military History* (New York: Oxford University Press, 1999), s.v. "Vietnam War (1960-1975): Causes," by Andrew J. Rotter.

[61] Ibid.

they had dropped a greater amount of high explosives in Vietnam than during the Second World War.[62]

In the North, things were more complicated. After Stalin's death in 1953, ideological differences drove the Soviet Union and China apart. According to Arbatov, one of these dealt with Chinese accusations of "betraying the revolutionary cause and the liberation movements."[63] Then in October, 1964, Beijing exploded its first nuclear weapon and Khrushchev was overthrown.[64] From 1965-68 Hanoi received hundreds of thousands of troops from Beijing and thousands of military advisors from Moscow.[65] Washington's intervention in the South may have "forced the Politburo's hand,"[66] but China's increasing influence in the region was another factor behind Soviet involvement.[67] Eventually Moscow's military buildup allowed the USSR to assume primary responsibility while Beijing withdrew after realizing that it had created a strong pro-Soviet ally on its own border.[68]

---

[62] Hobsbawm, 217.

[63] Georgi Arbatov, *The System – An Insider's Life in Soviet Politics* (New York: Times Books, 1992), 176.

[64] Dobrynin, *In Confidence*, 132.

[65] Lind, xii., 19.

[66] Zubok, 198.

[67] Harry Gelman, *The Brezhnev Politburo and the Decline of Détente* (Ithaca: Cornell University Press, 1984), 108.

[68] Lind, 29.

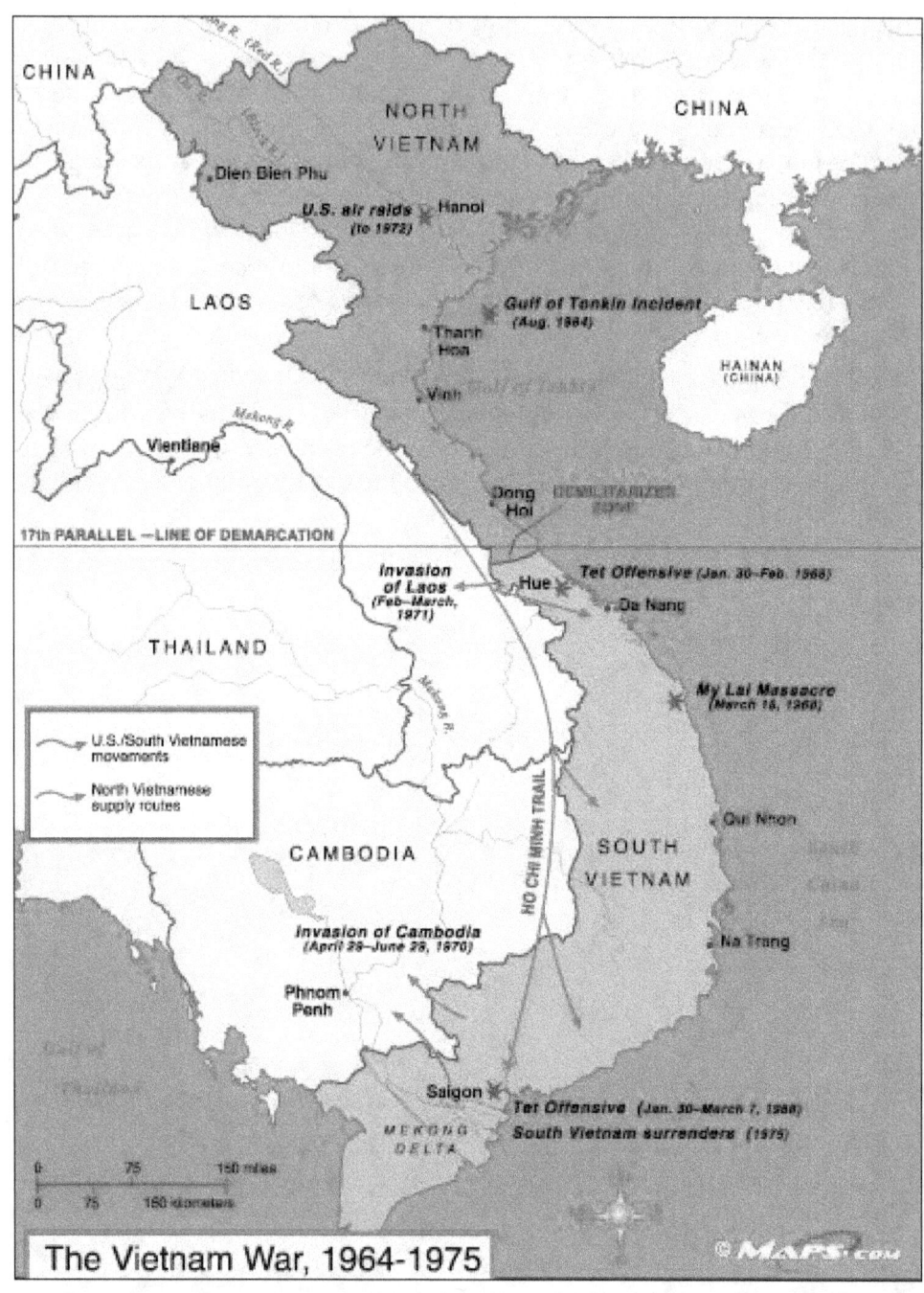

The Vietnam War, 1964-1975

Prior to the Vietnam War there had been a bi-partisan consensus, both in Washington and amongst the American electorate, supporting the Cold War doctrine of containment. Many Americans believed that halting the spread of communism around the world was the proper role for the United States. However, as early as 1966 Senator J. William Fulbright held several hearings of the Foreign Relations Committee debating the value of President Lyndon Johnson's policies in Vietnam and even containment itself.[69] Then in January, 1968, "the Vietcong's Tet Offensive exploded in living rooms across America."[70] Although the guerilla attack resulted in a communist defeat, the American military and people were completely caught off guard and disillusion set in. By 1974 a study reported that public concern in the US over war, communism, the strength of the military, and the Soviet Union had dropped significantly over the previous ten years.[71]

Many intellectuals who had formerly supported containment grew skeptical of the policy as well. Theologian Reinhold Niebuhr, historian Arthur M. Schlesinger, Jr., and economist John Kenneth Galbraith cited rifts between the Soviet Union and China as well as the different agendas of individual communist states as evidence that communism as an international conspiracy no longer existed.[72] Therefore, what sense did it make to have one uniform approach everywhere?[73] While others, including Norman Podhoretz of *Commentary* and William F. Buckley, Jr. of *National Review*, may have believed that America's exit from Vietnam demonstrated a loss of confidence in its role as leader of the free world, others argued that the US should never have aspired to play such a part in the first place.[74] Due to the length of the conflict, its location on the other

---

[69] Richard Gid Powers, *Not Without Honor – The History of American Anticommunism* (New Haven: Yale University Press, 1998), 321.
[70] Jay Winik, *On the Brink – The Dramatic, Behind-the-Scenes Saga of the Reagan Era and the Men and Women Who Won the Cold War* (New York: Simon & Schuster, 1996), 35.
[71] Ben J. Wattenberg, *The Real America: A Surprising Examination of the State of the Union* (Garden City, N.Y., 1974), 204; cited in Nelson, 21.
[72] Allen J. Matusow, *The Unraveling of America – A History of Liberalism in the 1960s* (New York: Harper & Row, 1984), 377, 378.
[73] Ibid., 378.
[74] Norman Podhoretz, *The Present Danger* (New York: Simon and Schuster, 1980), 30; William F. Buckley, Jr., *The Fall of the Berlin Wall* (Hoboken, New Jersey: John Wiley & Sons, Inc., 2004), 46; and Henry Kissinger, *Diplomacy* (New York: Simon & Schuster, 1994), 621.

side of the globe, as well as the enormous cost in blood and treasure, Americans became divided over whether all of the sacrifice had been worth it.[75]

Thus with the advent of the Nixon Administration the stated goal in Vietnam was to attain "peace with honor." This referred to an American withdrawal, but not before conditions had been achieved that would provide the South Vietnamese with at least a chance to survive alongside their communist rivals to the North. Nixon and Kissinger believed that a poorly maneuvered exit would damage American credibility and hamper the maintenance of international stability.[76] Thus they sought to exploit the Soviet-Chinese rivalry through "triangular diplomacy," (balancing the interests of China, the Soviet Union, and the United States[77]) while also understanding that neither Moscow nor Beijing directly controlled Hanoi.[78] Nixon and Kissinger linked progress in Vietnam to areas of Soviet interest, including arms control and trade. According to Kissinger, his first overture to Hanoi occurred before Nixon had even been inaugurated.[79] However, the North Vietnamese demanded an unconditional American withdrawal as well as the toppling of South Vietnamese President Nguyen Van Thieu's government in Saigon before they would release American prisoners of war.[80] For the Nixon White House, complete capitulation to an enemy and abandonment of an ally would certainly not have qualified as "peace with honor." Hence, in 1969 Kissinger and North Vietnamese Politburo member Le Duc Tho began private peace talks in Paris.[81]   These   were   in   addition   to   the

---

[75] For a more in depth and critical examination of the origins of American involvement in Vietnam as well as of Nixon's handling of the war see Gabriel Kolko, *Anatomy of a War – Vietnam, the United States, and the Modern Historical Experience* (New York: Pantheon Books, 1985); George C. Herring, *America's Longest War – The United States and Vietnam, 1950-1975*, third ed. (New York: McGraw-Hill, Inc., 1996); and Stanley Karnow, *Vietnam – A History*, second ed. (New York: Penguin Books, 1997).

[76] Richard A. Melanson, *American Foreign Policy Since the Vietnam War – The Search for Consensus from Nixon to Clinton* (Armonk, New York: M.E. Sharpe, 1996), 65.

[77] Jonathan Aitken, *Nixon – A Life* (Washington, D.C.: Regnery Publishing, Inc., 1993), 426.

[78] Garthoff, *Détente and Confrontation*, 250.

[79] Kissinger, *Diplomacy*, 678.

[80] Ibid.

[81] Stephen E. Ambrose, "The Christmas Bombing," in *The Cold War – A Military History*, ed. Robert Cowley (New York: Random House, 2005), 401.

official talks at Paris's Hotel Majestic, which included South Vietnam and the communist guerillas known as the Vietcong.[82]

Meanwhile in the backchannel, Kissinger sought Dobrynin's help in getting North Vietnam to come to an agreement. Kissinger said that Dobrynin frequently downplayed Moscow's influence on Hanoi.[83] This may have reflected Soviet fears that applying too much pressure on the North Vietnamese would drive them towards China, the Soviet Union's rival for the title of "leader" of the communist nations.[84] Moscow may have also been concerned that Hanoi would resent being asked to make concessions for the sake of US-Soviet détente.[85] Along with North Vietnam's insistence on an end to Thieu's regime, this could explain why negotiations dragged on for several years.[86]

According to Nixon, in early 1972 his administration received intelligence that large amounts of Soviet arms were pouring into North Vietnam.[87] Moscow may have been attempting to reassert its influence with Hanoi to spite Beijing after Nixon's visit there in February.[88] Then on March 30, 1972, North Vietnam initiated a full-scale invasion of the South.[89] South Vietnamese communist guerillas known as the Vietcong were joined by 120,000 troops of the North Vietnamese regular army equipped with Soviet tanks and artillery.[90] With the arrival of troops from Hanoi which were backed by Moscow, Kissinger argued that the notion of the Vietnam War as simply a popular uprising of guerillas in the South had been destroyed.[91] Despite a scheduled visit with Brezhnev later that month, on May 8 Nixon announced "Linebacker I," the bombing of North Vietnam and mining of Haiphong Harbor. The purpose was to halt further

---

[82] Kissinger, *Diplomacy*, 684.

[83] Henry Kissinger, *White House Years* (New York: Simon & Schuster, 1979), 266.

[84] Dimitri K. Simes, *Détente and Conflict: Soviet Foreign Policy, 1972-1977* (Washington, D.C.: Georgetown University, The Center for Strategic and International Studies, 1977), 21.

[85] Gelman, 108, 109.

[86] Richard Nixon, *RN – The Memoirs of Richard Nixon* (New York: Grosset & Dunlap, 1978), 583, 584.

[87] Ibid., 586.

[88] Ibid., 586.

[89] Garthoff, *Détente and Confrontation*, 257.

[90] Aitken, 436.

[91] Kissinger, *White House Years*, 1097.

delivery via rail or ship of military supplies from Moscow.[92] The first American-Soviet summit since 1961 was in great jeopardy.[93]

According to Dobrynin, the Politburo was divided over how to proceed. Defense Minister Marshall Andrei Grechko wanted the meeting cancelled, Foreign Minister Andrei Gromyko desired to press forward, and Chief Party Ideologist Mikhail Suslov remained undecided.[94] Arbatov claimed that KGB Chief Yuri Andropov told him privately that there had been great pressure on Brezhnev to punish Nixon by cancelling.[95] Some Politburo members were convinced that if the Soviets went ahead with the summit, "we would be politically humiliated and would lose our authority in the eyes of the world, particularly the Communist world, and with liberation movements," wrote Arbatov.[96] He believed that in the end Moscow forged ahead because it did not want to disrupt several pending agreements with the Federal Republic of (West) Germany, an American ally.[97] However, Dobrynin claimed that Moscow chose to hold the summit because "the alternative would amount to handing Hanoi a veto over our relations with America."[98]

The Chinese-Russian rivalry must be factored in as well. Nixon's visit to Beijing in February may have intensified Soviet fears of a Chinese-American alliance.[99] Thus Moscow, desiring a top-level meeting of its own more than ever, may have been more inclined to look the other way on American military activities in Vietnam.[100]

Kissinger and Dobrynin also deserved credit for the summit proceeding as scheduled. Both well understood the complexity of conducting superpower diplomacy while simultaneously supporting one's allies. Just prior to Nixon's bombing announcement, Kissinger asked to see Dobrynin.[101] (Dobrynin noted that whenever Kissinger asked to see him before Nixon was going to make a speech he knew bad news was

[92] Aitken, 437.
[93] Arbatov, 183.
[94] Dobrynin, *In Confidence*, 253.
[95] Arbatov, 183.
[96] Ibid.
[97] Ibid., 184.
[98] Dobrynin, *In Confidence*, 253.
[99] Nancy Bernkopf Tucker, "China as a Factor in the Collapse of the Soviet Empire," *Political Science Quarterly*, Vol. 110, No. 4 (Winter, 1995-1996), 503.
[100] Ibid.
[101] Kissinger, *White House Years*, 1187.

coming![102]) Upon hearing of Nixon's plans the Soviet ambassador was clearly disappointed.[103] Two days later when Dobrynin arrived at the Map Room of the White House, Kissinger held his breath out of fear that Moscow might cancel the summit.[104] Instead, Dobrynin merely read a note from his government registering what Nixon called "a relatively mild and private protest," with no mention of cancelling.[105] The next day over lunch Dobrynin told Kissinger, "You have handled a difficult situation uncommonly well."[106] He also credited Kissinger with understanding how difficult it was for the Soviets to proceed while their allies were being bombed by the Americans.[107]

Following the successful summit in May, on June 30th Kissinger spoke to Dobrynin from California to explain that Hanoi was attempting to gain leverage by injecting American domestic politics into the peace process:

K: Okay. Two things - - One, about the Vietnam talks. I wanted to say one thing about your friends there.

D: Where?

K: Hanoi. And I must say it very seriously to your leadership. One is they're already starting again what we told you at great length we would never tolerate.

D: What namely?

K: Well, now they've made a statement today saying they have forced us back to the conference table.

D: Henry, you know I mentioned to you the other day when we went over this, some kind of statement they will do it. They didn't specifically tell us what kind of statement.

---

102 Ibid.
103 Ibid., 1188.
104 Nixon, 607.
105 Ibid.
106 Nixon, 607; Kissinger, *White House Years*, 1194.
107 Dobrynin, *In Confidence*, 254.

K: Now they've invited Joe Kraft and some Labor leaders to Hanoi.

D: Joe Kraft?

K: Yeah. And you know what the purpose of this is.

D: No.

K: You know, they are going to float whatever proposals they're going to make publicly before they speak with us.

Then later...

K: If they play domestic politics here, we will do what we did in May. We will break off and escalate because we have nothing to lose that way. Then we will have to try to force them to their knees...I mean, I am telling you frankly. This is not to be transmitted in quite this brutal language.

D: Yeah, I understand. Well, the only thing we should really put in the promise is what you said in the middle. I mean, if they are really going to tell everything to all the people who come to them having nothing to do with the Administration and just give out publicly, then there is no sense to negotiate. ...Yeah, this I am prepared to ask on your behalf of my people in Moscow to tender to Hanoi. This I could do.[108]

Kissinger believed that Hanoi was not negotiating honestly. If this continued, he threatened that the US might intensify its aerial strikes. Dobrynin said that he understood and would relay the message to Moscow, but also politely explained that he would omit the part where Kissinger pledged to "force them to their knees."[109]

---

[108] [May-June 1972. Box #27.] *Henry A. Kissinger Telephone Conversation Transcripts (Telcons): [Anatoly Dobrynin File].* Richard Nixon Presidential Library and Museum, Yorba Linda, California. National Archives and Records Administration.
[109] Ibid.

On July 6 Kissinger again phoned Dobrynin from the West coast. Hanoi had extended an invitation to yet another American from outside of the administration – Labor leader James Hoffa.[110] "…sometimes Hanoi is beyond my comprehension," said Kissinger, adding "…it isn't even dangerous to us except that it's awfully hard to see how they can be serious if they keep doing idiotic things like this."[111] "No, I understand this, but sometimes in their own way of thinking this is very difficult to…Do you understand?" asked Dobrynin.[112] "Yeh, well, it's not a major thing," said Kissinger, who later expressed a greater concern:

> K: …Look, we're not going to bring a new negotiator in now – they're stuck with me. Because I'm afraid if I let them get away with it you'll ask me for a new negotiator.
>
> D: I don't want a new negotiator except for you.
>
> K: OK. Thank you.[113]

Although Kissinger had previously stated that the White House would "break off and escalate,"[114] in response to Hanoi's latest tactics, now he said "it's not a major thing."[115] Dobrynin, who often seemed to have a calming effect on the more animated Kissinger, had successfully made the case that this was just the way the North Vietnamese negotiated. By this time, Kissinger seemed much more concerned that negotiations between him and Dobrynin would continue as before.

As the presidential campaign of 1972 played out through the summer and into the fall, Nixon looked to be in an excellent position for re-election. The bombing and mining campaign in North Vietnam as well as triangular diplomacy appeared to be paying off. The last American combat troops were withdrawn from the North on August 12 as part of Nixon's Vietnamization policy (reducing the American role while increasing that of the South Vietnamese).[116] Later that month, *Nhan Dan*,

---

[110] [July 1972-September 1972. Box #27.]
[111] Ibid.
[112] Ibid.
[113] Ibid.
[114] [May 1972-June 1972. Box #27.]
[115] [July 1972-September 1972. Box #27.]
[116] Garthoff, *Détente and Confrontation*, 259.

a publication of the North Vietnamese Communist party, complained about the effects of the bombing while expressing frustration that Moscow and Beijing had abandoned the proletarian cause in favor of pursing détente with Washington.[117]

Consequently, the White House had leverage in its talks with North Vietnam. In early October, Kissinger and Le Duc Tho reached a tentative settlement around four agreements: a ceasefire, a return of prisoners-of-war, a total American withdrawal from South Vietnam, and the creation of a National Council of Concord and Reconciliation.[118] The membership of the council would be drawn in three equal parts from the existing South Vietnamese government, communists, and neutrals, with the assigned task of setting up elections.[119] Remarkably, Hanoi had dropped their long-standing demand for an end to Thieu's government in Saigon.[120] Although there were several remaining issues, perhaps the most difficult problem would be getting Thieu to accept an agreement which gave the communists a political role and permitted more than 150,000 North Vietnamese troops to remain in the South.[121]

On the morning of October 15 Kissinger explained to Dobrynin that the White House viewed the presence of these North Vietnamese regular army units in the South, as well as the flow of Soviet arms to them, as the main obstacles to getting South Vietnam to settle.[122] Since the administration had no interest in a confrontation with Saigon so close to the November 7 election, Kissinger inquired if the Soviets could intercede with Hanoi to obtain a partial withdrawal.[123] "We recognize they can't pull them all out, but if there could be at least some token movement and most importantly the question of military supplies to them. And what the President wants to do is write a letter to Brezhnev," said Kissinger.[124] "I understand. This is just for his [Brezhnev's] consideration," replied Dobrynin.[125] Although Dobrynin met with Kissinger later that afternoon to receive Nixon's letter, the Soviet ambassador said that since the

---

[117] Ibid.

[118] Ambrose, 402.

[119] Ibid.

[120] Kissinger, *Diplomacy*, 691.

[121] Ambrose, 402.

[122] [October 1972. Box #27.]

[123] Ibid.

[124] Ibid.

[125] Ibid.

ongoing negotiations were between Washington and Hanoi it would be "premature" for Moscow to make any promises about reducing weapons shipments to North Vietnam.[126] However, he would pass along the request in regard to North Vietnamese troop withdrawal.

This exchange demonstrated how Soviet cooperation was not only essential to get the North Vietnamese to negotiate, but also to enable the US to make progress with its own ally in the South. At times, Kissinger seemed to view Saigon as being just as intransigent as Hanoi, and claimed that without some North Vietnamese troop withdrawal it would take much longer to come to an agreement.

From May 9 until October 23, 1972, the US made 41,500 aerial attacks on North Vietnam,[127] but on October 24 Kissinger told Dobrynin that the White House would stop all bombing north of the 20th parallel as long as negotiations continued.[128] The following day the White House was prepared to go further. Although Hanoi requested Kissinger to visit North Vietnam, he believed that would alienate Saigon. Instead, he offered a halt to all bombing of North Vietnam if Le Duc Tho would meet him in Paris for further negotiations.[129] Kissinger told Dobrynin to inform Moscow that Washington's offer had come as a direct result of a positive message from the Kremlin the day before in regard to how "issues of prestige should not stand in the way when peace is so near."[130]

However, on October 26 North Vietnam publicly announced the tentative agreement reached earlier that month between Washington and Hanoi.[131] This was almost certainly a tactic to apply pressure on Saigon and portray Thieu as an obstructionist to peace.[132] Perhaps against his better judgment, Kissinger felt compelled to confirm the story by announcing, "'We believe peace is at hand.'"[133]

Richard Nixon was overwhelmingly re-elected in a 49 state landslide on November 7, 1972. The outcome had implications far beyond the President's personal political fortunes, however. It ensured

---

[126] Dobrynin, *In Confidence*, 266.

[127] Garthoff, *Détente and Confrontation*, 259.

[128] [October 1972. Box #27.]

[129] Ibid.

[130] Ibid.

[131] Stephen F. Hayward, *The Age of Reagan – The Fall of the Old Liberal Order, 1964-1980* (Roseville, CA: Prima Publishing, 2001), 371.

[132] Ibid., 372.

[133] Ibid.

that Soviet-American relations would continue with the Kissinger-Dobrynin backchannel as the main point of contact. The next day, Dobrynin relayed the congratulations of the Soviet government. Although it is tempting to dismiss this as just polite diplomacy, it is highly probable that the Soviets were genuinely pleased by the result of the contest between Nixon and South Dakota Senator George McGovern, for it guaranteed that they would be dealing with the same administration – at least for a while. As usual, Kissinger found it hard to be humble:

> D: Good morning, Henry.

> K: We didn't carry Siberia.

> D: Oh. My impression on the contrary, [you] carried all my country because even now in my Embassy I am listening "Four more years, four more years."

> K: Is that what you're saying?

> D: Exactly. In my Embassy everybody is shouting with beginning four years this 12 o'clock at night. So I hear even from Moscow the same - - I mean, the same sounds…

Then later…

> D: Well, once again, Henry, from deep in my heart I really like this development because I really have a very nice relationship - -

> K: I don't know whether one can have a feeling of personal friendship with a Communist diplomat but I have it.

> D: (laughter) So my best personal regards towards you and to the President. Please regard my personal regards too.

> K: Thank you.[134]

---

[134] [November 1972-December 1972. Box #27.]

Just as everything seemed to be progressing more or less smoothly towards an end to the war, the North Vietnamese launched a renewed offensive on the South in late November. Hanoi had lost patience with Saigon's refusal to settle and was outraged that Kissinger had recently visited South Vietnam, but skipped the North. On November 26, Kissinger gave Dobrynin the news in his typically colorful way:

K: Well, your friends have gone crazy.

D: I look at things…and I figure that Thieu – you couldn't handle him from this point of view. You know from both sides I don't need to tell you because you know them probably the best because you have a chance to observe them…from a short distance. I only from a long distance.

K: Right. Well, where we are – you know I don't know what influence you have over them [Hanoi]. We will give a rather moderate response…

Then later…

K: It's very stupid because if they had followed what we told them there would certainly have been an agreement in three weeks.

D: Well, you see I think one of the reasons was that they really wanted you to come there [to Hanoi]... I still don't see – well I know your reasons.

K: Because it would have led to an explosion in Saigon.[135]

Dobrynin believed that Kissinger had made a tactical mistake by snubbing the North Vietnamese: "They have really high emotions . . . . . in Hanoi. This I can tell you quite frankly."[136] To which Kissinger replied, "I've told them again and again that I would have to get the approval of Saigon and elsewhere. They just always said no…"[137] Once again, a mutual

---

[135] Ibid.

[136] Ibid.

[137] Ibid.

understanding of the complexity of engaging in superpower détente while also seeking to mollify one's allies was apparent. Kissinger and Dobrynin had been over this before, and though they still disagreed, each was able to appreciate the other's position.

A couple of days later, Kissinger discovered that the Soviet embassy was asking questions about his future. Although Nixon had just been re-elected, it was not a foregone conclusion that all of his various cabinet advisors would be retained. On November 28, 1972, Kissinger assured Dobrynin that he had nothing to worry about:

> K: Well, I read in the papers that you people are inquiring whether I'm on the way out.
>
> D: Who inquired?
>
> K: I saw a newspaper article saying officials of the Soviet Embassy made inquiries all over town last week.
>
> D: Oh, I think it was just, you know, sometimes the press just try to make up things. It's important that I know that you are in, no doubt.
>
> K: I'm relaxed.
>
> D: Yes, so there is not any problem.[138]

Although he dismissed the press reports, Dobrynin conceded that it was important to him that Kissinger would be around and that the partnership would continue. This exchange and others like it reveal the comfort and even a degree of dependence between Kissinger and Dobrynin which developed over time. Such a relationship helped to promote trust, a willingness to give the benefit of the doubt, and forbearance during trying situations.

Over the next several weeks, the American and North Vietnamese delegations continued negotiations to put the final touches on a settlement. However, Thieu still refused to agree to a ceasefire as long as North

---

[138] Ibid.

Vietnamese forces remained in the South.[139] In early December Kissinger travelled to Paris to convince Le Duc Tho to remove the troops, but he refused and the talks once again broke down.[140] When Kissinger returned to Washington on December 13 he explained the situation to the White House.[141] Nixon believed he had to show Saigon that he would come to its rescue if Hanoi violated the ceasefire, as well as show Hanoi the price they would pay for such a violation.[142] On December 14 he decided on another round of full-scale bombing.[143]

The renewed bombing campaign, "Linebacker II," targeted shipyards, radio transmitters, armaments factories, and military bases.[144] Hanoi utilized Soviet surface-to-air missiles (SAMS) in defense.[145] After 729 flights by B-52 bombers and 1,800 sorties overall in eleven days,[146] (with a thirty-six hour break during Christmas[147]) on December 29 the North Vietnamese agreed to reopen talks.[148] Kissinger and Le Duc Tho then met in Paris on January 8, 1973, to begin final negotiations to end the Vietnam War.[149]

Mark Clodfelter argued that Nixon succeeded where Johnson had failed in using air power because the nature of the war had changed.[150] When Johnson personally conducted his "Rolling Thunder" campaign from 1965-68, the US was primarily fighting Vietcong guerillas.[151] Due to the hit and run nature of guerilla warfare in which prolonged engagements were avoided, the Vietcong did not require long supply lines which could be destroyed by bombing.[152] However, after the American defeat of the Vietcong during the Tet Offensive of 1968, the war became a

---

[139] Ambrose, 402.

[140] Ibid.

[141] Ibid.

[142] Ibid., 403.

[143] Hayward, 373.

[144] Aitken, 455.

[145] Ambrose, 403.

[146] Morris, 350.

[147] Ambrose, 409.

[148] Reed, 153.

[149] Dobrynin, *In Confidence*, 268.

[150] Mark Clodfelter, *The Limits of Air Power – The American Bombing of North Vietnam* (New York: The Free Press, 1989), 205.

[151] Ibid.

[152] Ibid.

more traditional conflict with Hanoi's regular army.[153] A large army was more exposed to the effects of bombing, thus Nixon's "Linebacker I" and "Linebacker II" campaigns of 1972 had greater impact.[154]

According to a discussion between Kissinger and Dobrynin on January 16, 1973, one of the sticking points prior to the most recent round of bombings had been Hanoi's insistence on linking the release of American prisoners of war to the release of political prisoners held by Saigon.[155] Kissinger rejected the notion that the release of American POWs should be contingent on South Vietnam's actions. After the "Christmas bombing," however, Hanoi agreed to release American POWs within two months of signing a treaty.[156] Meanwhile, the US promised to "use its influence" in getting political prisoners released from Saigon.[157] Remaining issues included Hanoi's request for $5 billion in compensation as a result of the recent bombing and the removal of mines.[158]

There had also been progress with South Vietnam. Thieu finally gave his assent to the agreement even though it permitted North Vietnamese troops to remain in the South.[159] In several letters, Nixon assured Thieu that aid would be resumed if needed, but also threatened to abandon the South Vietnamese President if he did not settle.[160]

On January 22, 1973, Kissinger spoke with Dobrynin just before embarking for Paris to sign a peace accord to end the Vietnam War.[161] The conversation revealed a sense of anticipation, but also uneasiness due to so many past disappointments:

> AD: Talk about protocols - - does - - is it all right everything in Paris?
>
> HK: We have a few minor problems, but it's inconceivable they'll hold us up. We need from them a very, very minor concession as a face-saving thing for Thieu - -

---

[153] Ibid., 206.

[154] Ibid.

[155] [January 1973-February 1973. Box #27.]

[156] Ibid.

[157] Ibid.

[158] Ibid.

[159] Ambrose, 414.

[160] Ibid., 413.

[161] [January 1973-February 1973. Box #27.]

AD: On protocol?

HK: On protocols and they are so minor - - they are all crazy - - the Vietnamese are crazy so you can't assume it will be done, but that's only the real problem. It's so complex - - you have to be half Vietnamese to understand it.

AD: But I gather now you are more than half Vietnamese. . . .

HK: Oh I am. It is inconceivable that the thing will not succeed now.

AD: They may prolong for two-three days.

HK: An extra day, but

AD: In this case when you are going to initial it should be by this time [on] Monday [or] Tuesday - - everything should be initialed by this time?

HK: We would like to initial everything together because once you let these maniacs loose, it's going to start all over.

Then later…

AD: Well, good luck, Henry.

HK: Thank you Anatol and I need not tell you what a joy it has been to work with you. . .seriously we have done a lot of good things together.

AD: Yes, Right. Henry.

HK: It took us two and a half years really to get started in the last administration - - this one we can start with a running start.[162]

Kissinger and Dobrynin must have felt vindicated when representatives of the US, North Vietnam, South Vietnam, and the Vietcong signed the Paris Peace Accords on January 27, 1973.[163] They hoped to accomplish even more during Nixon's second term.

However, by the spring of 1973 the accords were already unraveling. According to Kissinger, North Vietnam had maintained forces in Laos and Cambodia, moved eleven of its twelve divisions into South Vietnam in early 1975, and obtained military equipment well in excess of agreed-upon replacement levels – all violations of the Paris agreement.[164] Indeed, Moscow *increased* military shipments to Hanoi throughout 1974 and 1975.[165] Meanwhile, the US Congress ended funds for any American military purposes in Indochina in June, 1973.[166] US economic aid to Saigon also declined from $2.3 billion in 1973, to $1.1 billion in 1974, and to $700 billion in 1975.[167] It must have been a bitter pill for Kissinger after his efforts to obtain "peace with honor." A Nobel Peace Prize had followed for him and Le Duc Tho in 1973, but it could stop neither the North Vietnamese offensive nor the flow of Soviet military equipment in support of it.

What of Dobrynin? What role did he have in Moscow's actions? Although he may have approved of the developments in Vietnam, it is highly doubtful that he had anything to do with effectively sabotaging his work with Kissinger. The walls between the various Soviet government bureaucracies made it unlikely that an ambassador in the Foreign Ministry had knowledge of the Defense Ministry's plans or activities. Additionally, Dobrynin often differed with his superiors on matters of policy as in the

---

[162] Ibid.

[163] John Whiteclay Chambers II, ed. *The Oxford Companion to American Military History* (New York: Oxford University Press, 1999), s.v. "Vietnam War (1960-1975): Military and Diplomatic Course," by David L. Anderson.

[164] Henry Kissinger, *Crisis – The Anatomy of Two Major Foreign Policy Crises* (New York: Simon & Schuster, 2003), 422.

[165] Gelman, 164.

[166] H.W. Crocker, III, *Don't Tread On Me – A 400-Year History of America at War, from Indian Fighting to Terrorist Hunting* (New York: Crown Forum, 2006), 378; Kissinger, *Diplomacy*, 696.

[167] Morris, 351.

case of emigration restrictions. It seems probable that he would have preferred for Moscow to be less egregious in the way it assisted Hanoi.

After receiving intelligence that Saigon could only hold on for another three or four weeks, President Ford addressed a joint session of Congress on April 10, 1975.[168] Although Kissinger advised the President to blame Congress and even wrote a "'go down with the flags flying'" speech,[169] Ford opted for a more conciliatory approach. He requested $722 million in military aid and $250 million more for economic and humanitarian assistance.[170] However, when he met with the Senate Foreign Relations committee on April 14th, Senators Jacob Javits of New York, Frank Church of Idaho, and Joseph Biden of Delaware (the future Vice-President) only pledged support for evacuating Americans.[171]

In a highly redacted conversation from April 18, 1975, Kissinger and Ford discussed the possibility of obtaining a ceasefire in order to stage an evacuation.[172] "I called in Dobrynin tomorrow morning. I want to ask him for a temporary cease-fire to permit evacuation of Americans and Vietnamese," said Kissinger.[173] "Do they have control or the power to effect a cease-fire?" inquired Ford.[174] "No probably not," replied Kissinger, "but I want to ask him not to ship any military equipment during that time. I am for taking the 2 chances in 20 that they may help…"[175]

Ford then implied that congressional limitations on the Central Intelligence Agency had helped to precipitate the crisis: "No President including myself, can operate with a crippled intelligence community. It doesn't make sense to destroy the agency for one mistake they made."[176] Of course, it had been more than one mistake. CIA director William E. Colby later handed over to Congress an institutional study revealing hundreds of cases of civil liberties abuses at home as well as excesses in

---

[168] Gerald Ford, *A Time to Heal* (New York: Harper & Rowe, 1978), 253.

[169] Ibid., 253, 254.

[170] Ibid., 254.

[171] Ibid., 255.

[172] Kissinger Transcripts. Department of State. Available at http://foia.state.gov/SearchColls/CollsSearch.asp.

[173] Ibid.

[174] Ibid.

[175] Ibid.

[176] Ibid.

covert activities abroad over the life of the organization.[177] CIA personnel referred to the warrantless wiretaps, assassination plots and break-ins as the "Family Jewels."[178] Following investigations by a presidential commission as well as special committees of both the House and Senate, the agency's reputation became badly tarnished by the end of the 1970s.[179]

On April 24, Dobrynin relayed a message from Brezhnev through the backchannel: "The position of the Vietnamese side on the question of evacuation of American citizens from South Vietnam is definitely positive...they have no intention to put any obstacles in the course of military actions to the evacuation of American citizens from South Vietnam..."[180] Washington had received Moscow's assistance in obtaining time to stage an evacuation. Hanoi had said that it would not interfere.[181] Nevertheless, two days later Dobrynin received a message from Ford stating that the North Vietnamese were bombarding the Saigon airport as well as several buildings in the vicinity of the American embassy.[182] When Kissinger charged Hanoi with seeking to humiliate Washington, Dobrynin cited complaints in Congress and the media that the American evacuation had taken too long.[183] As the end drew near, more than 6,000 Americans and South Vietnamese escaped from the roof of the embassy as helicopters made repeated trips to off-shore Navy ships to rescue them.[184] Saigon fell on April 30, 1975.

Following the North Vietnamese takeover, thousands of South Vietnamese were executed and tens of thousands imprisoned.[185] Over the next few years, more than one million people fled Indochina as South Vietnam, Cambodia, and Laos all fell to communist regimes.[186] Hundreds of thousands became refugees as "boat people,"[187] risking their lives on barely sea-worthy vessels with many coming to the United States.

---

[177] G.J.A. O'Toole, *Honorable Treachery – A History of U.S. Intelligence, Espionage, and Covert Action from the American Revolution to the CIA* (New York: The Atlantic Monthly Press, 1991), 492.

[178] Ibid.

[179] Ibid.

[180] Kissinger Transcripts. Department of State.

[181] Hayward, 406.

[182] Dobrynin, *In Confidence*, 349.

[183] Ibid.

[184] Hayward, 406.

[185] Morris, 351.

[186] Crocker, 379.

[187] Ibid.

A united Vietnam was just one of ten new communist regimes which emerged around the world from 1974-1980.[188] To what extent was this driven by Moscow? On the other hand, could there have been a "bandwagoning effect" or "'psychological domino effect'" leading countries to align with the seemingly ascendant Soviet Union?[189] Certainly for those viewing the Cold War as a global "zero-sum reputational game," Moscow was winning and Washington was losing.[190]

The October 1973 Arab-Israeli/Yom Kippur War

Ever since the creation of the modern state of Israel in 1948, war or the threat of war between the Jewish nation and its Arab neighbors has been an almost constant feature of international headlines. After the Israeli War of Independence in 1948-49, subsequent conflicts occurred during the 1956 Suez Canal Crisis and the 1967 Six Day War. The last of these resulted in Israel obtaining the Golan Heights from Syria, the West Bank of the Jordan River from Jordan, and the Sinai Peninsula and Gaza Strip from Egypt. American support for Israel and Soviet backing of Egypt and Syria ensured that the Arab-Israeli conflict intersected with détente.

The Soviets established a relationship with the Egyptians as early as 1955 when Khrushchev and Egyptian President Gamal Abdel Nasser completed an arms agreement.[191] According to Kissinger, in the 1960s Moscow was the main arms supplier to both Egypt and Syria and provided organization and technical assistance to radical Arab groups.[192] By the 1970s support for national liberation on the one hand and a desire to pursue détente with the Americans on the other forced the Soviets to walk a fine line.

---

[188] Dinesh D'Souza, "How Reagan Won the Cold War," *National Review*, 24 November 1997, 39; (South Vietnam, Cambodia, Laos, South Yemen, Angola, Ethiopia, Mozambique, Grenada, Nicaragua, and Afghanistan).

[189] Lind, 49.

[190] Ibid., 29.

[191] Parker, 348.

[192] Kissinger, *Diplomacy*, 737.

As the foremost ally of Israel (the Americans had been first to recognize the Jewish state in 1948 under President Harry S. Truman), the US would oppose efforts to re-arm Cairo and Damascus. Consequently when Nasser's successor, Anwar Sadat, requested new arms shipments, the Soviets insisted on being paid with hard currency which they knew the Egyptians did not have – thus preventing a sale in 1972.[193] In a move to assert his independence, Sadat expelled approximately 20,000 Soviet military advisors in July of that year.[194] This also could have been a shrewd attempt to compel the Soviets to come through on the promised deliveries.[195] When Saudi Arabia provided Egypt with five hundred million dollars in January, 1973, Moscow was forced to make the weapons

---

[193] Richard D. Anderson, Jr., Margaret G. Hermann and Charles Hermann, "Explaining Self-Defeating Foreign Policy Decisions: Interpreting Soviet Arms for Egypt in 1973 through Process or Domestic Bargaining Models?" *The American Political Science Review* Vol. 86, No. 3 (Sep., 1992), 761.

[194] Simes, *Détente and Conflict: Soviet Foreign Policy, 1972-1977*, 23.

[195] Gelman, 153.

transaction.[196] While the Soviets probably did not want a confrontation with the Americans, they did seek the enhanced prestige in the developing world which a successful Arab war to reclaim lost territories would bring.[197]

Saturday, October 6

On October 6, 1973 – the Jewish holy day of Yom Kippur – Sadat and Syria's Hafiz Al-Assad initiated a coordinated attack on two fronts. The Egyptians used makeshift pontoon bridges to send 70,000 troops and 800 tanks across the Suez Canal into the Israeli-occupied Sinai Peninsula.[198] Meanwhile, the Syrians invaded the Golan Heights.[199] At 9:20 a.m. Kissinger explained the situation on the ground to Dobrynin:

> K: Our information is that the Egyptians and Syrians have attacked all along their [fronts] and also. . .
>
> D: Is it the canal.
>
> K: The Canal and the Golan Heights. [Egyptian Foreign Minister] Zayyat is claiming the Israelis launched a naval attack on some isolated spot in the Gulf of Suez and that triggered the whole thing.
>
> D: I saw on a ticker they claim that Israel began attack. Zayyat told you.
>
> K: He told me not along the Canal but in the Gulf of Suez. We are all going to have to be taking formal positions. You and I know that is baloney if they [the Israelis] are going to attack they will not launch an attack in the Gulf of Suez and at the key points. Not their style.
>
> D: I understand.

---

[196] Anderson, Herman, and Herman, 762.

[197] Simes, *Détente and Conflict: Soviet Foreign Policy, 1972-1977*, 24.

[198] Hayward, 417.

[199] Ibid.

K: How is it that the Syrians and Egyptians are starting at the same minute - - all along the front. If it started with an Israel naval attack, you and I are having a problem in how to get this stopped. We are using our maximum influence with the Israelis to show restraint...

D: O.K. I will send additional message to Moscow. Really madness.

K: Total madness...We should meet urgently. We should, I think use this occasion to first not to have everything we have achieved destroyed by maniacs on [either] side and after quieting it down to see what can be done constructively.

D: All right. Thank you very much.[200]

It must have been infuriating for Kissinger and Dobrynin to contemplate that all of their work in building détente could potentially be undone by the Arab-Israeli dispute. However, as events unfolded both would take the opportunity to advance his country's interests through support of respective allies. The tension between conducting superpower diplomacy and simultaneously pursuing security, economic, and ideological goals in the Middle East would test the Kissinger-Dobrynin relationship as never before.

Kissinger probably believed that going before the entire United Nations General Assembly, including numerous Arab and Soviet bloc nations, would be too time consuming and result in a less favorable outcome for the United States and Israel. The UN Security Council, which included only the US, Soviet Union, China, France, and Great Britain as permanent members, would be a much more hospitable environment. Around 7:00 p.m. Kissinger pressed for a Security Council ceasefire resolution, but Dobrynin explained why his government was opposed:

D: ...I had rather hear from Moscow but as I understand our position the difficulties we are now facing is that the

---

[200] Kissinger Transcripts. Department of State.

Arabs are trying to regain the lands occupied by Israel. They have been using that argument to us and for us to tell them you cannot free your land, it is ridiculous.

K: I recognize the situation. I am not saying it is all easy. We have a different situation. There have not been any raids on Damascus and Cairo but I would not bet anything on tomorrow.

D: I understand.

K: Is [it] possible for the Politburo to imagine a complete course of action which we agree on privately.

D: What course of action do you propose besides SC [Security Council].

K: A defacto return to the status quo ante a defacto return of the ceasefire...

D: I understand.

K: We have a framework out of which we could crystallize. The Arabs have now proved their point.

D: Henry, how could they?

K: You see they are going to lose. It is not a case where we are asking. Not like [the 1971 war between] India and Pakistan.

D: I understand. The military point of view. I cannot argue with you. You know the situation better. I am trying to understand the situation better politically.[201]

Both diplomats seemed convinced that it was just a matter of time until the Israelis repelled the Egyptians and Syrians. For this reason, Kissinger

---

[201] Ibid.

explained that there was no point in the Arabs continuing their offensive. In fact, he intimated that if a ceasefire did not come soon Cairo and Damascus might become vulnerable.

Kissinger and Dobrynin knew that the way they handled the situation would have repercussions beyond the Middle East. Détente had opponents in both of their countries, and a poor outcome would play right into the hands of its critics. "If you and we could find a way of settling this now then it would be an overwhelming argument in all of the things we have been going through as to what the practical consequences have been of our relationship," said Kissinger.[202] "I understand," said Dobrynin, but since the Soviets had proclaimed their support for the ideological goal of national liberation they felt constrained in what they could do: "They [the Arabs] would say you have spoken of liberating. It is impossible for us."[203]

Monday, October 8

At 8:30 a.m. Israel launched a counterattack.[204] The prospect of the superior Israeli military pushing back the Arab gains must have induced a change of heart in Moscow. At 9:54 a.m. Dobrynin told Kissinger, "We have contacted the leaders of the Arab states on the question of ceasefire. We hope to get a reply shortly."[205] Kissinger replied that the White House would hold off submitting a resolution before the Security Council for the time being and settle for "a general discussion" instead.[206]

Tuesday, October 9

Thus far the only Arab nations involved in the conflict were Egypt and Syria. However, Dobrynin seemed genuinely shocked when Kissinger told him at 11:29 a.m. about a message the White House had just received from the Kingdom of Jordan:

---

[202] Ibid.

[203] Ibid.

[204] Richard C. Thornton, *The Nixon-Kissinger Years – The Reshaping of American Foreign Policy*, 2nd ed. (St. Paul, Minnesota: Paragon House, 2001), 264.

[205] Kissinger Transcripts. Department of State.

[206] Ibid.

K: "The Soviet Charge [*d'Affaires*] asked to see King [Hussein] and was received this morning. Charge said Soviets fully support Arabs in conflict with Israel. He said Soviet Union thought all Arab States should enter battle now."

D: Soviet, what?

K: "Soviet Union thought all Arab . . ."

D: Soviet Union?

K: Yes.

D: Thought or fought?

K: Recommending to the King.

D: Un-huh.

K: "King considers this a Soviet request for him to send his army into action.."

D: We asked King to go into action?

K: Yeah.[207]

"Unbelievable story," replied Dobrynin.[208] And truly it was. If the Soviets had encouraged other Arab countries to join the fighting rather than pressuring Egypt and Syria to agree to a ceasefire as they had claimed, it could have meant the death-knell for détente. Dobrynin desperately sought a clarification: "Was it ours . .? I don't have any information at all...our support of Arab countries is nothing new. But as you said we asked King to send.........yes?"[209] After Kissinger told him

---

[207] [October 1973. Box #28.]

[208] Ibid.

[209] Ibid.

that he had heard correctly, the bewildered Dobrynin said he would check with Moscow immediately.[210]

Brezhnev had indeed sent a message to the other Arab nations. But why take such a chance of damaging détente? The answer lies in the fact that two separate Soviet foreign policy goals came into conflict with the outbreak of hostilities in the Middle East. To the Arab world, Israel represented a Western implant and the latest incarnation of European colonialism, somewhat similar to South Africa.[211] The past partnership of Tel Aviv and Johannesburg in some military matters and even the production of nuclear weapons only added to this perception.[212] The USSR had to demonstrate its commitment to national liberation and preserve its influence in the region by assisting the Arabs.[213] However, if it appeared that the Israelis faced destruction, the US would intervene and Moscow wanted to avoid a confrontation with Washington which could jeopardize détente.[214] Consequently, on October 9 the Soviets initiated an arms airlift to Egypt and Syria.[215] But in order to limit the Soviet role, Brezhnev also sent a letter to President Boumedienne of Algeria exhorting all of the Arab nations to join the fight.[216] The Soviets sought to provide enough help to prevent an Arab defeat, but not so much that Egypt and Syria would achieve a total victory over Israel.[217]

Wednesday, October 10

At 8:13 a.m. the next morning, Dobrynin had an update from Moscow on the ceasefire question.[218] The Soviets decided that their relationship with their allies prohibited them from supporting such a measure, however, they would not oppose one either – the Soviet representative on the Security Council would abstain during voting.[219] This was a logical position for the Soviets to take as they sought a middle ground between preserving détente and upholding the principle of national

---

[210] Ibid.

[211] Glenn E. Perry, *The Middle East – Fourteen Islamic Centuries* (Upper Saddle River, New Jersey: Prentice Hall, 1997), 279.

[212] Ibid.

[213] Ulam, 106.

[214] Ibid.

[215] Ibid.

[216] Ibid.

[217] Ibid.

[218] [October 1973. Box #28.]

[219] Ibid.

liberation. Kissinger said he would need time to discuss it with Nixon, but gave Dobrynin permission to tell the Kremlin that it had been "a constructive message."[220]

Later that morning domestic politics put the Middle East on hold. Vice-President Spiro Agnew had been investigated for months by the Justice Department on charges of bribery, extortion, and tax fraud dating from his time as Governor of Maryland.[221] He eventually pled no contest to a single count of tax evasion, and was about to resign.[222] Therefore the White House was unable for the time being to respond to the Soviet abstention proposal. At 11:45 a.m. Kissinger confided in Dobrynin:

> K: Anatol, I just wanted to tell you something. We are having a major domestic problem, which as you will see, even you will recognize it's major, which is coming to a head early this afternoon.
>
> D: Yeah.
>
> K: And so there will be decisional delay until I can get you - - But you will get your formal answer.
>
> D: You mean it happens today or tomorrow?
>
> K: By the end of the day I will give you an answer.
>
> D: By the end of the day.
>
> K: I just want you to know. You will see that this is not a delaying tactic.
>
> D: Yeah. But what is the crisis? Could you tell me that?
>
> K: Well, it concerns the Vice President.
>
> D: Oh, I see.

---

[220] Ibid.

[221] Aitken, 503.

[222] Ibid., 504.

K: So I wanted you to know that and I'll be in touch with you around 4:00 or 5:00 o'clock this afternoon.[223]

Now it was Dobrynin's turn to be patient. Kissinger closed by saying, "Now what I've told you about this domestic situation, Anatol, is a sign of my great confidence in you."[224] "No, no, no. I understand," replied Dobrynin.[225]

But by 5:40 p.m. the White House had still not replied.[226] "We consider it a serious proposal and we have to think this thing through to think how to answer," explained Kissinger.[227] Dobrynin seemed more concerned about a potential American airlift to Israel: "Henry, I see in the news media...build-up."[228] To which Kissinger answered, "For your information, we are doing next to nothing."[229] Kissinger then appealed to Dobrynin on a personal level: "Anatoly, you have gone through too many crises with me. We are trying to get this thing settled. You are going to hear from us during the course of the evening."[230] He also explained that as Secretary of State he had to sign all government commissions as well as receive all resignations.[231] Dobrynin seemed to understand the need for Kissinger's involvement in Agnew's departure.

At 9:45 p.m. Kissinger told a disappointed Dobrynin that there had been too much happening during the day for the White House to respond to the Soviet proposal to abstain.[232] Dobrynin could be forgiven for thinking that he was now the one being strung along. When he pressured Kissinger, the truth finally came out. The Soviet decision to abstain from the ceasefire vote "did not fill us with ecstasy," admitted Kissinger.[233] "Well, nothing really...nothing followed after this," Dobrynin replied.[234] Support for rival Middle Eastern nations was straining détente as well as the Kissinger-Dobrynin relationship.

---

[223] Kissinger Transcripts. Department of State.
[224] Ibid.
[225] Ibid.
[226] Ibid.
[227] Ibid.
[228] Ibid.
[229] Ibid.
[230] Ibid.
[231] Ibid.
[232] [October 1973. Box #28.]

[23³] Ibid.
[234] Ibid.

Saturday, October 13

At 7:55 p.m. Kissinger confronted Dobrynin about an ongoing Soviet airlift: "...we cannot not supply our friends while you are supplying yours."[235] He claimed that up to that point no American planes had landed in Israel.[236] (According to Richard C. Thornton, Kissinger was telling the truth; although the Israelis had been asking for help for three days, the White House had resisted out of fear that an airlift would lead to an overwhelming Israeli victory and thereby destroy Washington's role as an international peacemaker.[237] Benny Morris speculated that Tel Aviv may have applied pressure by threatening to resort to nuclear weapons if the Israelis ran out of conventional arms.[238]) Then on an ominous note for détente, a frustrated Kissinger asked: "Why do we have to deal with you,...why not deal with Sadat directly[?]"[239] Dobrynin answered that it was "Up to you and the President to decide," but that it could have "disastrous results."[240]

Sunday, October 14

The following afternoon at 12:36 p.m., Kissinger told Dobrynin that the US had started airlifting supplies to the Israelis.[241] It would stop as soon as a ceasefire was declared if the Soviets would also halt their airlift to the Arabs.[242] Kissinger also reiterated the dangers to détente posed by the ongoing situation, and Dobrynin likewise had a warning in regard to their conversation the previous evening:

K: You know, Anatol, we all know now what is at stake because if this goes on much longer, ...

D: Well,_____if you had a chance to read my telegram [to Moscow] what I sent yesterday it was exactly what I am told. [by Kissinger]

---

[235] Ibid.

[236] Ibid.

[237] Thornton, 267.

[238] Benny Morris, *Righteous Victims – A History of the Zionist-Arab Conflict, 1881-2001* (New York: Vintage Books, 2001), 434.

[239] [October 1973. Box #28.]

[240] Ibid.

[241] Ibid.

[242] Ibid.

K: No, no I….

D: I make my own reservations of course, but it was a direct quotation everything you said. It is not only fair, but it is important for them to know the mood. At a certain point of our usual thing, I don't do direct quotations, but a summary, I make it. But yesterday I was rather in a detail of what you said because this is what I feel…[243]

Normally Dobrynin simply summarized his discussions when he reported to Moscow. Indeed Kissinger probably owed him a debt of gratitude for censoring some of the Secretary of State's more bombastic rhetoric over the years. However, Dobrynin deemed Kissinger's threat to deal directly with Sadat and thereby cut Moscow entirely out of the peace process as serious enough to merit a direct quote to the Kremlin.

Tuesday, October 16
As tensions neared the breaking point, word came from Oslo that Kissinger and Le Duc Tho had been honored with the Nobel Peace Prize for their efforts at ending the Vietnam War. At 11:42 a.m. Dobrynin offered his congratulations:

D: I hope I will be invited to the party.

K: What party?

D: Which you are going to give in connection with the award of the Nobel Prize.

K: I figure it like Groucho Marx said, "Any club that took him in, he does not want to join." I would say anything that Le Duc Tho is eligible for there must be something wrong with it.

Then later…

---

[243] Ibid.

D: It does not matter about the present difficulties. I am sure we will come out of this - - both of our countries...

K: ...I don't see what you and I, our countries, can gain in the Middle East compared to what we can lose and therefore we cannot let these maniacal parties drive us into confrontation.

D: This is the reason I am calling you. To congratulate you. This is for the second prize.

K: Right.

D: *For the second Nobel Prize for you next year.*

K: *Good. We will aim for that.*[244] (italics mine)

The effect of past diplomatic successes on Kissinger and Dobrynin should not be underestimated. Their shared experiences with SALT, Vietnam, and elsewhere provided reassurance that they would overcome the current crisis in the Middle East as well.

Friday, October 19

During an epic tank battle on the Sinai Peninsula, the Israelis drove between the Egyptian Second Army in the north and the Third Army in the south, eventually reaching the western side of the Suez Canal.[245] The Third army was in danger of being completely surrounded and annihilated.[246] Only the depleted First Army remained to protect Cairo.[247] If the Israelis scored another overwhelming victory as in 1967, Soviet influence in the Middle East could be destroyed.[248] For a change, Kissinger let Dobrynin do most of the talking as the latter read a message from Brezhnev to Nixon at 11:04 a.m.:

D: "Dear Mr. President:

---

[244] Kissinger Transcripts. Department of State.

[245] Perry, 277.

[246] Ulam, 109.

[247] Perry, 278.

[248] Ulam, 109.

The events in the Middle East become more and more dangerous. Our two powers, as we have both agreed, must do the utmost in order to keep the events from going beyond the limits, when they could take even more dangerous turn."

K: Right.

D: "If they develop along this way there is a danger that harm could be done even to the immediate relations between the Soviet Union and the United States. We believe that neither you, nor we want to see it…"

K: Right.

D: "Since time is essential and now not only every day but every hour counts,"

K: Right.

D: "my colleagues and I suggest that the US Secretary of State and your closest associate Dr. Kissinger comes in an urgent manner to Moscow to conduct appropriate negotiations with him as with your authorized personal representative. It would be good if he could come tomorrow, October 20. I will appreciate your speedy reply.
Sincerely, L. Brezhnev, October 19, 1973"

K: You are friendly, aren't you?

D: Hum?

K: That's a friendly suggestion.

D: Of course it is.[249]

---

[249] Kissinger Transcripts. Department of State.

Despite the tense situation, Kissinger obviously enjoyed teasing Dobrynin about the formal manner in which he sometimes conducted himself. Half an hour later after conferring with Nixon, Kissinger said that the White House had agreed "in principle" to accept the Soviet invitation.[250] "Will you come back there [to Moscow] with me," asked Kissinger.[251] "Yes, if you don't mind I would like to go both ways," Dobrynin replied.[252] "Well, as long as you sit in the front compartment," joked Kissinger.[253] "All right. I would rather sit in the tail but nevertheless," laughed Dobrynin.[254]

The ongoing international crisis was occurring simultaneously with a domestic constitutional crisis,[255] further demonstrating the importance of the backchannel. The day after the above conversation was October 20, 1973 – date of the so-called "Saturday Night Massacre." Watergate Special Prosecutor Archibald Cox had demanded the full release of the White House tapes concerning the Watergate break-in.[256] Nixon offered to provide summaries of the tapes instead of transcripts, but Cox refused.[257] When Nixon ordered Attorney General Elliot Richardson to fire Cox, Richardson refused and resigned.[258] When Deputy Attorney General William Ruckelshaus also refused to fire Cox, he was fired.[259] Finally, Solicitor General Robert Bork agreed to remove Cox.[260] Nixon had acted decisively in coming to the aid of the Israelis, but he was no longer in any position to handle international affairs.

Kissinger's visit to Moscow was successful. On Sunday, October 21, he and Brezhnev drafted a cease-fire proposal.[261] At 12:52 a.m.[262] (Washington time) on Monday, October 22, the UN Security Council passed resolution #338 sponsored by both the US and USSR calling for a

---

[250] [October 1973. Box #28.]

[251] Ibid.

[252] Ibid.

[253] Ibid.

[254] Ibid.

[255] *Nixon*, produced by David Espar, Elizabeth Deane, and Marilyn Mellowes, 170 min., WGBH Educational Foundation, 1990, DVD.

[256] Aitken, 507.

[257] Nixon, 931.

[258] Aitken, 508.

[259] Ibid.

[260] Ibid.

[261] Nixon, 936.

[262] Garthoff, *Détente and Confrontation*, 372.

ceasefire.[263] But before returning to Washington, Kissinger accepted the request of Prime Minister Golda Meir to first stop in Israel.[264] While there he intimated that the Israelis need not comply with the ceasefire at the exact time that it was supposed to go into effect, twelve hours after adoption.[265] He had given tacit permission for Israel to continue fighting, a move which would have grave consequences shortly thereafter.[266]

Wednesday, October 24

"Anatol, the madmen in the Middle East seem to be at it again," Kissinger lamented at 9:45 a.m.[267] Israeli activity had supposedly ceased on the west bank of the Suez Canal, but now Israel was claiming that the Egyptians were attacking them on the east bank.[268] Kissinger told Dobrynin that the US had warned both sides to stop any offensive actions.[269] Then at ten after ten in the morning, Kissinger said that the US was sending in its military observers from Tel Aviv to verify that the Israelis were only making defensive moves.[270] Perhaps sensing Dobrynin's concern, Kissinger reminded his colleague of what was at stake: "Now the important thing is for you and us to stay together having made this historic achievement [the ceasefire]."[271] "Now this is the point," replied Dobrynin.[272] Five minutes later Kissinger reported that according to the Israelis all fighting had ceased.[273] He added that the US would send ten military observers to the battle zone for about forty-eight hours until the UN observers arrived.[274]

What transpired over the next several hours would draw the United States and the Soviet Union closer to war than at any time since the Cuban Missile Crisis of 1962. Around 1:00 p.m. Sadat sent Nixon a message accusing the Israelis of violating the cease-fire.[275] Shortly thereafter, the

---

[263] Ulam, 109.

[264] Thornton, 274, 275.

[265] Ibid.

[266] Ibid., 275.

[267] [October 1973. Box #28.]

[268] Ibid.

[269] Ibid.

[270] Ibid.

[271] Ibid.

[272] Ibid.

[273] Ibid.

[274] Ibid.

[275] Kissinger, *Years of Upheaval*, 579.

Egyptian government announced that it was seeking a Security Council meeting to request US and Soviet troops be sent to the Middle East.[276] This was the last thing Kissinger wanted, particularly in such a potentially explosive region. In his words, "The makings of a crisis were appearing."[277]

At 3:35 p.m. that afternoon, Dobrynin read a telegram from Soviet Foreign Minister Andrei Gromyko.[278] Egyptian and Soviet sources were claiming that fighting was continuing on the Israeli side: "Therefore, information given by Israel to the White House is Israel stop fighting is false," read Dobrynin.[279] "Please immediately inform Dr. Kissinger of the false information and put information before the President," he added.[280]

By 7:00 p.m. Washington time, the Soviet leadership decided that more extreme measures were warranted.[281] The Israelis had completely surrounded the Egyptian Third Army on the Sinai Peninsula, leaving little in the way of a direct assault on Cairo.[282] Likewise, Damascus was threatened on the eastern front.[283] Moscow could not allow their Arab clients to be defeated again, consequently the Soviets instructed their UN representative to support a resolution directing American and Soviet troops to the war zone, provided someone else (presumably Egypt) introduced it.[284] At 7:25 p.m. Kissinger spoke to Dobrynin and the day's tensions boiled over:

> K: I have been talking to the President and we really want to urge you not to push matters to an extreme because we will veto any resolution that calls for sending over any military forces. What we need is more observers.

---

[276] Ibid.

[277] Ibid.

[278] Kissinger Transcripts. Department of State.

[279] Ibid.

[280] Ibid.

[281] Kissinger, *Years of Upheaval*, 581.

[282] Ulam, 110.

[283] John Whiteclay Chambers II, ed. *The Oxford Companion to American Military History* (New York: Oxford University Press, 1999), s.v. "Middle East, U.S. Military Involvement In The," by Douglas Little.

[284] Kissinger, *Years of Upheaval*, 581.

D: ...I mentioned to you when I was in Moscow it was completely out of the question to send any troops. Now they have become so angry they want troops.

K: Why through us. What was [would be] achieved?

D: *You allowed the Israelis to do what they wanted.*

K: *When this operation started I pleaded with you to get people to return from the lines and it took a week.*

D: *It* [the ceasefire] *was already agreed upon by you and Brezhnev....*

K: *Be that as it may, if you want confrontation we will have to have one...*

D: *You know we don't want to have a confrontation.*

K: *It is inevitable that there will be mutual charges in the first 24 hours of a ceasefire. We introduced two joint resolutions....*[285] (italics mine)

Kissinger correctly stated that the US had sought a ceasefire as soon as hostilities broke out and while Israel was on the defensive. He was also probably correct that there would be a few residual skirmishes after a ceasefire went into effect (leaving out that he may have encouraged such activities). Nevertheless, although the Soviets had initially resisted a ceasefire, now that the Arabs were on the defensive Moscow wanted it enforced.

The Soviets sent another letter to Washington at 9:35 p.m.[286] "Kissinger sounded nervous as I read to him Brezhnev's message over our confidential telephone line," wrote Dobrynin.[287] The Soviets were threatening to act even if the US did not join them in enforcing the ceasefire.[288] Kissinger proceeded to call an emergency meeting of the

---

[285] Kissinger Transcripts. Department of State.

[286] Garthoff, *Détente and Confrontation,* 376.

[287] Dobrynin, *In Confidence,* 301.

[288] Garthoff, *Détente and Confrontation,* 377.

Washington Special Actions Group (WSAG) for 10:30 p.m.[289] At 10:15 p.m. he told Dobrynin that the White House was reviewing the latest Soviet offer:

> K: We are assembling our people to consider your letter. I just wanted you to know if any unilateral action is taken before we have had a chance to reply that will be very serious.
>
> D: Yes, all right.
>
> K: This is a matter of great concern. Don't you pressure us. I want to repeat again, don't pressure us!
>
> D: All right.[290]

The discovery by U.S. intelligence that the Soviets had mobilized and put seven airborne divisions on alert further indicated that the situation had truly reached a crisis point.[291]

Fearing imminent, unilateral military action by the Soviets to enforce the ceasefire, the US put its forces on a DefCon3 or "Defense Condition" world-wide nuclear alert at 11:41 p.m.[292] Some alleged that Nixon made the move to distract attention from his ongoing tug-of-war with Congress over the White House tapes.[293] However, due to the President's distraction with Watergate, it was Kissinger who led the White House meeting, issued the alert, and generally handled the crisis in the Middle East.[294]

The Soviet threat to intervene drove the Americans to pressure Israel to stop its advance and allow the Third Egyptian Army to be resupplied.[295] Concerned that if the Israelis achieved a total victory they

---

[289] Kissinger, *Years of Upheaval*, 585.

[290] [October 1973. Box #28.]

[291] Hayward, 418-419.

[292] Kissinger, *Years of Upheaval*, 587, 588; On a descending scale from 1 to 5, DefCon 1 means war.

[293] Ulam, 111.

[294] Johnson, 668.

[295] Tompson, 45.

would refuse to return any of the occupied territories, Kissinger threatened to cut off military aid unless Tel Aviv accepted a ceasefire.[296]

Thursday, October 25

Cooler heads eventually prevailed. The next morning at 5:40 a.m., the White House sent a letter to Brezhnev with an offer to send US and Soviet observers as well as UN forces.[297] At 3:40 p.m. Dobrynin called Kissinger with Brezhnev's reply:

K: Anatoly?

D: Hello Henry. I would like to read to you a letter from Brezhnev to the President and then I will send you...

K: Is it going to calm me down or make me go into orbit again?

D: No, not orbit...Prefer to stay in orbit quietly...[reading Brezhnev's letter] Since you are ready now, as we understand it, now to send to Egypt a group of American observers, we agree to it jointly in this question. Soviet group of observers instructed to get into contact immediately in a businesslike operation with the US group of observers...[298]

After Dobrynin finished reading the letter Kissinger said, "I thought you were threatening us. Don't ...I take threats very badly. We will talk about it sometime."[299] Dobrynin agreed, "No, [it] isn't anything to discuss now..."[300]

A potential disaster had been narrowly averted. But what caused this colossal misunderstanding? The success of détente thus far had been in large part due to a sense of trust and empathy built up over several years between Kissinger and Dobrynin. Established practice had been that

---

[296] Iwan W. Morgan, *Beyond the Liberal Consensus – A Political History of the United States Since 1965* (New York: St. Martin's Press, 1994), 79.

[297] Garthoff, *Détente and Confrontation*, 380; Kissinger, *Years of Upheaval*, 591.

[298] [October 1973. Box #28.]

[299] Ibid.

300 Ibid.

nothing was said publicly or even at the traditional diplomatic level without first being discussed in the backchannel. The last thing Dobrynin heard was at 10:15 p.m. on Wednesday the 24th when Kissinger said the White House was considering the Soviet offer. Nothing else had been forthcoming until 4:00 a.m., and even then no mention was made of putting the country on an alert.[301] The prospect of Soviet ground forces in the Middle East shocked the White House, leading Nixon and Kissinger to believe that past diplomatic procedure no longer applied. The absence of communication through the backchannel represented a breakdown in the process and almost proved fatal for relaxing tensions.

Saturday, October 27

At 11:24 a.m. Kissinger and Dobrynin finally had an opportunity to discuss at greater length the disaster which had almost occurred over the previous couple of days:

> K: We had the impression that you were planning a military move. We did not invent this. Someday soon we have to discuss this. We had no reason to meet until 4:00 in the morning.

> D: …On this, I think, one thing was really a big blunder on your [side], maybe it was deliberate. For six hours you are just telling us every hour to wait, there will be a reply. I am sure if you had just mentioned to me that the President feels it was necessary to make an alert…[and] blow up our relations…

> K: That was a blunder.

> D: Seven hours you were telling us [to wait] and then we receive a letter that didn't say a word about the alert. It was widely publicized.

> K: Whether you ever believe it or not it is not important now. I am telling you it was not…we were convinced you

---

301 Ibid.

were planning something unilateral. We were as [outraged]. We thought the tone in that letter....

D: You were pretty sure we would do it. If you were so sure, you could have waited one hour to get some additional information from Brezhnev. But you didn't want to have it.

K: That isn't true. I was very tough. [I said] Don't pressure us. I sent you two or three messages to please don't do anything unilateral.

D: Exactly.

K: You could have said what makes you think we will do anything unilateral. We have no intention of taking action.

D: What you said was to wait for a reply. I sent four telegrams to Moscow -- this was a unique situation -- to wait for a reply from the President. What did they receive...Someday in Moscow...much more easy to discuss.

K: We very truly thought you were threatening us out of the....

D: Exactly, you have it with us. Wait for the reply. By the way nothing was said...[302]

Kissinger seemed regretful for what he admitted had been "a horrible misunderstanding."[303] He also sought to repair the personal relationship: "Too much is at stake for us to be angry with each other."[304] Dobrynin said that he had only been angry "for two days," but that anger in Moscow

---

[302] Ibid.

[303] Ibid.

[304] Ibid.

was "still very high."[305] He claimed that Kissinger later admitted that calling the alert had been a mistake.[306]

The October 1973 Arab-Israeli/Yom Kippur War had several long-term effects. First, the Soviets removed any doubt that they could deliver arms and supplies around the world in a relatively short time.[307] This had implications for further interventions throughout the 1970s. Second, in 1973 eleven of the Organization of Petroleum Exporting Countries (OPEC) instituted an oil embargo on nations deemed too friendly to Israel, including the US.[308] When the embargo ended the next year, OPEC had increased oil prices by three hundred percent, contributing to inflation throughout the decade.[309] As a leading oil-exporting nation, the Soviet Union benefitted from the higher petroleum prices, allowing Moscow to increase military spending at the same time that Washington was reducing its by about fifty percent.[310] However, the amount of wealth that the Soviets obtained from petroleum and natural gas also served as a disincentive to developing other sources of economic vitality through science and technology.[311]

Were détente and the Kissinger-Dobrynin relationship vindicated during the October War? Both had complicated matters by prolonging the fighting when their respective allies appeared to have the upper hand.[312] Kissinger admitted that détente "had not prevented a crisis," and that both Washington and Moscow attempted to "reduce the role and influence" of the other.[313] However, he also explained that détente "defined not friendship but a strategy for a relationship between adversaries."[314] Dobrynin argued that the Soviet Union and the United States "cooperated in bringing the war to an end," but likewise conceded that they "sought to manipulate events to serve their own ends and to extend their own influence in the Middle East."[315] Although he believed that both nations wanted to prevent the war from affecting their relationship, he suggested

---

[305] Ibid.

[306] Dobrynin, *In Confidence*, 305.

[307] Tompson, 45.

[308] Morgan, 79.

[309] Ibid.

[310] Gaddis, *The Cold War*, 212.

[311] Arbatov, 215.

[312] Garthoff, *Détente and Confrontation*, 369.

[313] Kissinger, *Years of Upheaval*, 600.

[314] Ibid.

[315] Dobrynin, *In Confidence*, 292.

that Kissinger was "prepared to use and even sacrifice this relationship to reduce and if possible eliminate Soviet influence in the Middle East under the cover of détente."[316]

To some extent Kissinger was successful. By forcing Israel to retreat when Cairo appeared about to fall, the US showed Sadat that it could apply pressure on its ally.[317] Thereafter the US and Egypt resumed diplomatic relations on November 7 after a six-year hiatus.[318] Kissinger's "shuttle diplomacy" then resulted in the Egyptians and Israelis signing a cease-fire agreement on November 11 and returning to the positions they had occupied on October 22.[319] Subsequent agreements in January, 1974, and September, 1975, resulted in partial Israeli withdrawals from the Sinai.[320] Kissinger also oversaw an agreement in May, 1974, whereby the Israelis partially withdrew from the Golan Heights in Syria.[321]

Eventually it was President Carter who helped engineer a long-term Egyptian-Israeli peace at Camp David in September, 1978.[322] By signing the *Camp David Accords* in 1979 and acknowledging Israel's right to exist, Sadat regained the rest of the Sinai as well as earned a Nobel Peace Prize (with Israeli Prime Minister Menachem Begin.)[323]

Angola

The US-Soviet proxy war in Angola marked a crucial turning point for détente. After acquiring naval and air bases in South Yemen, Moscow enhanced its ability to intervene in Africa, which then emerged as a new battlefield in the Cold War.[324] As in Vietnam, Soviet actions were driven in part by competition with the Chinese, who by 1975 had established relationships with Zambia, Tanzania, Zaire, and Mozambique.[325]

---

[316] Ibid.

[317] Tompson, 45.

[318] Nixon, 943.

[319] Ian J. Bickerton and Carla L. Klausner, *A Concise History of the Arab-Israeli Conflict* (Upper Saddle River, New Jersey: Prentice Hall, 1998), 187.

[320] Ibid., 188, 189.

[321] Benny Morris, 439.

[322] Bickerton and Klausner, 187.

[323] Gaddis, *The Cold War*, 204.

[324] Henry Bienen, "Perspectives on Soviet Intervention in Africa," *Political Science Quarterly* Vol. 95, No. 1 (Spring, 1980), 36.

[325] Simes, *Détente and Conflict: Soviet Foreign Policy, 1972-1977*, 35.

Oil-rich Angola, a former Portuguese colony for 500 years,[326] represented another of the revolutionary movements on the continent which were either communist or nationalist and shared Moscow's disdain for Western imperialism.[327] Soviet economic and military aid, protection, and "political models" were some of the benefits of this common outlook.[328] Arbatov classified such direct military assistance to liberation movements as an example of Soviet "errors and political miscalculations, which were strongly in evidence from the mid-1970s on."[329] He also described the policy as "loaded with revolutionary jargon and closely intertwined with imperial ambitions."[330] Soviet foreign policy specialist Andrei M. Alexandrov even likened Angola to the Spanish Civil War of the 1930s, and believed intervening represented "our internationalist duty."[331]

Dobrynin suggested that Angola "raised the question of whether détente had any general rules outside our mutual behavior toward each other, and if so, what they were."[332] For Kissinger the issue was not Marxism.[333] He claimed that when Mozambique gained independence from Portugal under the Marxist Front for the Liberation of Mozambique (FRELIMO), Washington extended recognition and established diplomatic relations.[334] However, he viewed Angola as problematic because it represented "the projection of Soviet military power into Africa."[335]

According to Dobrynin, the International Department of the Communist Party of the Soviet Union (CPSU) used the Portuguese Communist Party (PCP) to first establish contact with and then provide support to the Angolan liberation movement.[336] One of the most reliably obedient parties to Moscow, the PCP had backed Soviet actions against

---

[326] Yanek Mieczkowski, *Gerald Ford and the Challenges of the 1970s* (Lexington, Kentucky: The University Press of Kentucky, 2005), 285; Morgan, 80.

[327] Daniels, 160.

[328] Ibid.

[329] Arbatov, 193.

[330] Ibid.

[331] Ibid., 195.

[332] Dobrynin, *In Confidence*, 365.

[333] Henry Kissinger, *Years of Renewal* (New York: Simon & Schuster, 1999), 794.

[334] Ibid.

[335] Ibid.

[336] Dobrynin, *In Confidence*, 367.

Finland in 1939 and the invasion of Hungary in 1956.[337] In the 1950s the PCP created the Popular Movement for the Liberation of Angola (MPLA).[338] Thus it is possible that the Angolan revolution in 1959 was initiated by Moscow and carried out at least in part by the PCP.[339] Alongside the rebellion against colonial rule, the pro-communist MPLA and the anti-communist National Union for the Total Liberation of Angola (UNITA) had fought a civil war since the early 1960s.[340]

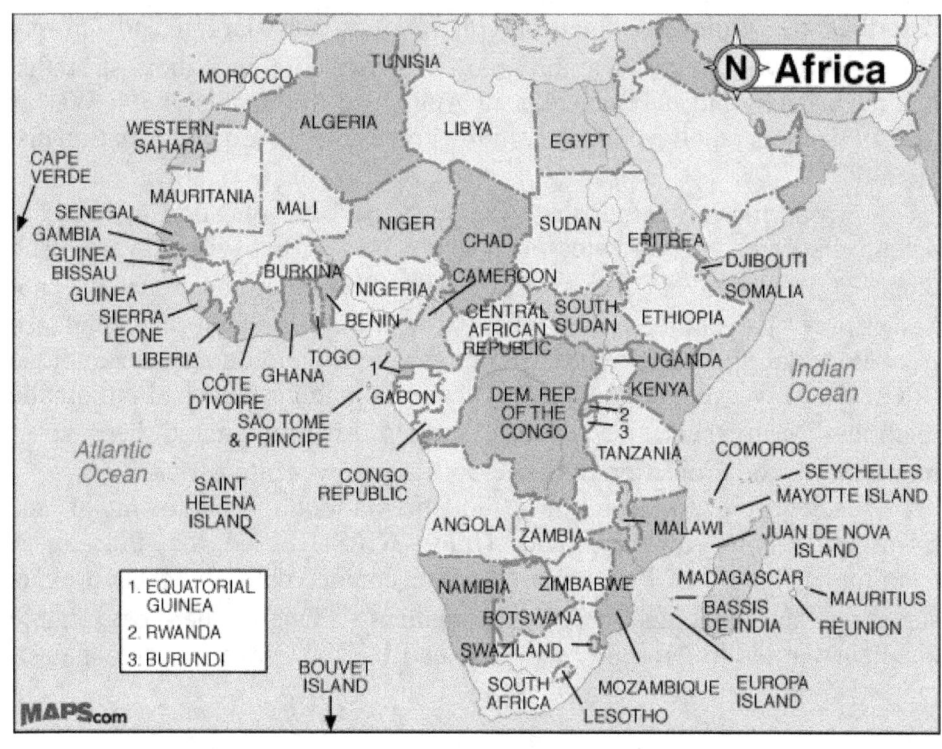

1974 was a pivotal year in the fortunes of Angola. On April 25, the fascist regime of Antonio de Oliveira Salazar was overthrown in a military coup in Portugal.[341] General Antonio Spinola led the new

---

[337] Brian Crozier, *The Rise and Fall of the Soviet Empire* (Rocklin, California: Prima Publishing, 1999), 233.

[338] Ibid.

[339] Ibid., 233, 234.

[340] Ibid., 234.

[341] Ibid., 236.

government.[342] which included Alvaro Cunhal, a PCP leader who in February had been honored with the Order of the October Revolution while in Moscow.[343] In June, Portugal and the Soviet Union established diplomatic relations.[344] The next month the Portuguese army withdrew from Angola.[345] Finally, in January, 1975, Angola's competing factions agreed to form a government and hold elections.[346]

However, fighting broke out before any votes could be cast. Predictably, the superpowers backed their respective ideological allies. The Soviets supported the MPLA, led by former medical student and convert to Marxism Agostinho Neto.[347] Meanwhile, the Americans adopted UNITA as well as a third group, the National Front for the Liberation of Angola (FNLA).[348]

Brezhnev believed that Soviet involvement in Angola was "just," but it also presented an opportunity to show China that the Soviet Union was still the leader of international communism.[349] Meanwhile Ford and Kissinger viewed American involvement as critical to re-establish US credibility after the loss of Vietnam.[350] The United States government believed that it had to respond to the further spread of communism around the globe.

Several events during 1975 prompted Ford and Kissinger to dramatically increase the US role in Angola. Sometime in the spring, perhaps as early as March, but probably no later than May, Cuban advisers arrived to train the MPLA in the use of Soviet tanks and weapons.[351] On April 17, Lon Nol's US-backed government fell to the communist Khmer

---

[342] Thornton, 358.

[343] Crozier, 236, 237.

[344] Ibid., 237.

[345] Yves Santamaria, "Afrocommunism: Ethiopia, Angola, and Mozambique," trans. Jonathan Murphy and Mark Kramer in *The Black Book of Communism*, ed. Stephan Courtois, et. al. (Cambridge, Massachusetts: Harvard University Press, 1999), 696.

[346] Robert M. Gates, *From The Shadows – The Ultimate Insider's Story of Five Presidents and How They Won the Cold War* (New York: Simon & Schuster, 1996), 66.

[347] Thomas J. Noer, "International Credibility and Political Survival: The Ford Administration's Intervention in Angola," *Presidential Studies Quarterly* Vol. 23, No. 4, The Managerial, Political, and Spiritual Presidencies (Fall, 1993), 772.

[348] Mieczkowski, 285, 286.

[349] Ibid., 286.

[350] Noer, 771.

[351] Santamaria, 697; Thornton, 369.

Rouge in Cambodia.[352] On April 19, Zambia's President Kenneth Kaunda requested Ford and Kissinger intervene in Angola to counter the Soviet Union and protect his and other African nations.[353] By the end of the month, Vietnam was united under a communist regime.[354] Later that summer, communists took complete control of Laos as well.[355] To some, these events showed that the tide was turning against US interests as more countries aligned with the Soviet bloc, particularly in the General Assembly of the United Nations.[356] For Gates, 1975 was "the worst year in CIA's history."[357]

Cuban involvement clearly affected Kissinger. He viewed those in the State Department and elsewhere who opposed intervention as suffering from "the Vietnam syndrome," referring to fears that US involvement would lead to a recreation of the long, drawn-out struggle in Southeast Asia.[358] He reasoned that a diplomatic solution would not be enough to counter the Soviets and the Cubans.[359] Consequently Ford and Kissinger increased military support to FNLA and UNITA from hundreds of thousands to millions of dollars.[360] Beginning in July, both factions received armored personnel carriers, surface-to-air anti-aircraft missiles, mortars, rifles, machine guns and other supplies and equipment from the CIA.[361] By September, the amount of aid had risen from an initial $14-$17 million to approximately $25 million.[362]

The introduction of Cuban combat troops was a crucial turning point in the Angolan intervention, détente, and the Cold War. Although the Cuban military had been involved in numerous African nations ever since Fidel Castro's communist revolution in 1959, previous military contingents usually never exceeded several hundred.[363] However, by the end of September at the latest, the first of thousands of combat troops from

---

[352] Johnson, 654.

[353] Kissinger, *Years of Renewal*, 791.

[354] Morgan, 81.

[355] Ibid.

[356] Lind, 55.

[357] Gates, 60.

[358] Noer, 775.

[359] Ibid.

[360] Ibid., 774, 775.

[361] Ibid., 776.

[362] Gates, 67.

[363] Thornton, 377.

Havana arrived in Angola.[364] Moscow had used military force in Eastern Europe, but Angola represented the first time Soviet military power had been applied (albeit through a proxy) into a civil war on the side of a pro-Soviet faction.[365]

Despite the increased US aid, Jonas Savimbi of UNITA claimed that he needed more. If Washington would not help, he threatened to appeal to apartheid South Africa, thus turning Angola into a diplomatic and public relations catastrophe.[366] Kissinger never admitted to working with South Africa, but according to the CIA there was communication and sharing of intelligence between Washington and Pretoria (Defense Minister P.W. Botha also reported that the US had asked for assistance.)[367] On October 14, South Africa invaded Angola in an attack on the Soviet-backed MPLA in the south, eventually reaching 500 miles inside of the war-ravaged country.[368]

For the sake of American credibility around the world, Ford and Kissinger believed that they had to press forward.[369] Since the amount in its contingency fund had fallen to a mere seven million dollars, the CIA sought Congressional approval.[370] However, agency director William Colby's testimony on November 6 before the Senate Foreign Relations Committee revealed that Congress had not been fully informed about either the extent or the details of US involvement in Angola.[371] Senator Dick Clark of Iowa, recently returned from a visit to the war-torn nation, declared that the CIA and White House had lied about the extent of the American role and charged that US actions had drawn Cuba and South Africa into the conflict.[372] California Senator John Tunney later sponsored the *Clark Amendment* cutting off CIA funding for covert operations in Angola,[373] adding "'I don't want to see any more money go down this rat hole.'"[374]

---

[364] Ibid., 378.

[365] Ulam, 134, 135.

[366] Noer, 776.

[367] Thornton, 381, 382.

[368] Noer, 776, 777.

[369] Ibid., 778.

[370] Ibid.

[371] Ibid., 777.

[372] Ibid., 777, 778.

[373] Ibid., 778.

[374] Mieczkowski, 287.

By November there were approximately 4,000 Cuban combat troops in Angola.[375] Although originally transported on Cuban planes and ships, that month the Soviets began providing long-range aircraft.[376] The MPLA took the capital of Luanda and declared the independence of the People's Republic of Angola on November 12.[377]

Meanwhile, Kissinger and Dobrynin worked in the backchannel, discussing the matter several times during October and November.[378] On December 9, Ford told Dobrynin that détente was being jeopardized by Soviet actions in Angola.[379] The next day the Soviets suspended their airlift,[380] and Kissinger and Dobrynin addressed the influx of arms from surrounding nations:

> K: …We cannot think of any other solution except to ask outside countries to promise not to send more arms in. If you are worried about the border in Zaire, we are willing to consider a UN force there. We promise you we would exercise restraint on our part and to get all foreign forces out.
>
> D: …The question really is in this case not very easy to control. It is in the capital of the country and no one knows where they are.
>
> K: But look it will be easily known if something comes in or not. If we don't keep our word, that will affect our relationship.
>
> D: Do you have any ideas if Africa could do something? It is their business. It is not natural for us really.
>
> K: No, but the way we could do it is to have the Organization of African Unity ask all outside powers, you see, and then we would both have an excuse to do it…

[375] Gates, 68.

[376] Garthoff, *Détente and Confrontation*, 512.

[377] Noer, 777.

[378] Garthoff, *Détente and Confrontation*, 522.

[379] Kissinger, *Years of Renewal*, 821.

[380] Ibid., 822.

However, there remained one wildcard:

> D: Who is going to control South Africa?

> K: We have nothing to do directly with South Africa, but we would bring major pressure on them.

> D: But if they continue?

> K: Look, we are trying to win. We are trying to get everybody out of it.[381]

Describing a mutual pullout as a "win" represented quite a lowering of expectations for Kissinger. He may have already given up hope of receiving further funding to displace the MPLA, and instead sought a face-saving measure to limit the damage to US prestige. Kissinger suggested to Dobrynin that if the US and the USSR would support an appeal from the Organization of African Unity to have all three factions begin talks, it could lead to a political solution.[382] Dobrynin seemed hesitant: "The question is themselves. Whether they are going to take this from us."[383] "I think if the two of us agree, we can get them to agree," replied Kissinger.[384]

A little over a week later, the *Clark Amendment* passed the Senate by a 54-22 vote on December 19.[385] An irate Ford lambasted the upper house: "'This abdication of responsibility by a majority of the Senate will have the gravest consequences for the long-term position of the United States and for international order in general.'"[386] The vote and leaked information concerning previous CIA covert activity in Angola may have encouraged the Soviets to step up their efforts.[387] After a brief pause from December 9 to 25, Moscow resumed its transport of Cuban arms and troops.[388]

---

[381] Kissinger Transcripts. Department of State.

[382] Ibid.

[383] Ibid.

[384] Ibid.

[385] Noer, 778.

[386] Ford, 346.

[387] Garthoff, *Détente and Confrontation*, 516.

[388] Ibid.

With the arrival of the election year 1976, a favorable outcome in Angola took on even greater importance for the White House. On January 3, Ford stated in an interview with NBC that Soviet actions in Angola violated the principles of détente.[389] On the 9th, Kissinger told Dobrynin that the lack of progress in Angola would force him to "make some bloody statements about the conditions…which can not be in your interest."[390] Kissinger seemed to be implying that the situation could affect his planned visit to Moscow to discuss the SALT II treaty as well as its chances for ratification thereafter. Dobrynin appeared threatened and the conversation grew tense:

> D: We are not…we have never considered it [Angola] a test of strength or will but you…

> K: No, it is on the part of Congress.

> D: *It has nothing to do with Congress…you are forcing this issue…We have to make a test of will between you and the Secretary General whether you will come if something happens in Angola?…Either Brezhnev has to agree to what Henry wants or the whole SALT issue is in the air.*

Then later…

> K: *I was hoping we could settle this thing quietly since neither of us have an overwhelming interest in Angola.*

> D: *Exactly. But you are forcing the point.*[391] (italics mine)

Perhaps no other conversation in the telcons better demonstrated the divergent views of the United States and the Soviet Union on détente. Kissinger insisted that the Soviets end their support for the MPLA, even after saying that Angola was of little strategic interest to the US. However, the White House believed Soviet and Cuban intent on aiding the MPLA made the country strategic. This exchange demonstrated how both

---

[389] Richard W. Stevenson, *The Rise and Fall of Détente – Relaxations of Tension in US-Soviet Relations, 1954-84* (Urbana and Chicago: University of Illinois Press, 1985), 175.
[390] Kissinger Transcripts. Department of State.
[391] Ibid.

superpowers viewed the outcomes of various conflicts in the developing world as indications of whose ideology was "winning." Ford and Kissinger were determined that Moscow would not "win" in Angola – not after Vietnam and especially not in an election year.

An increasingly frustrated Dobrynin then challenged Kissinger: "OK. You do it. You make a test. If you equate Angola to détente that is your business. If you feel it is that important, ok. We don't think it is...I will send to Brezhnev that you will have to take into consideration that you may not come because of Angola."[392] To which Kissinger responded, "No, I said that the conditions that are being created are not helpful ones," and "we trust that you are not working in a direction that during my visit things will happen that will be humiliating to the United States."[393] Although Kissinger eventually did travel to Moscow on January 20, 1976, there was no long-term agreement on Angola or SALT II.[394]

As expected, the House approved the *Clark Amendment* to the defense spending bill 323-99 on January 27, cutting off all CIA funding for Angola.[395] Although Ford supported the CIA's actions in Africa, he reluctantly signed the legislation in February because it also funded the B-1 bomber, the Trident missile, and the cruise missile.[396] The *Clark Amendment* would later be repealed during the Reagan administration[397] as part of a renewed effort in the 1980s to roll back communist gains.

By March of 1976 the MPLA emerged victorious.[398] At the end of 1977 there were 20,000 Cuban soldiers in Angola.[399] A conservative estimate of the cost of the Soviet intervention was $300 million, about ten times what the Americans spent, and this only included the cost of equipment – not troops.[400] The ability to fund such an operation indicated that the Soviet economy, while perhaps only 50-60% as large as that of the US, nevertheless could provide Moscow with numerous international opportunities. The Soviet Union had demonstrated to other liberation

---

[392] Ibid.

[393] Ibid.

[394] Thornton, 391.

[395] Noer, 780.

[396] Mieczkowski, 287.

[397] Kissinger, *Diplomacy*, 773.

[398] Tompson, 53.

[399] Nelson, 150.

[400] Gates, 68; Thornton, 391.

movements, the Chinese, and the Americans that it could intervene in support of its interests anywhere around the world.[401]

However, as Dobrynin explained the price for this victory was high because Angola "soured Americans on détente."[402] He claimed that the Soviet embassy attempted to tell Moscow that Washington viewed Angola as "a test of détente," but that these warnings went unheeded by "the morally self-righteous" in the Kremlin.[403]

Foreign interventions were the *coup de grace* for détente. Although the policy limped on for another few years into the Carter Administration, the Soviet invasion of Afghanistan in 1979 was the last straw. Through the backchannel, Kissinger and Dobrynin had established empathy and achieved numerous diplomatic successes. However, the telephone transcripts show that even at a détente, both the United States and the Soviet Union continued to view themselves as a nation and a cause, complicating the work of diplomacy. Ultimately, Kissinger and Dobrynin were unable to reconcile the conflicts between their respective national ideologies, and détente became little more than a short respite from the Cold War.

---

[401] Tompson, 53.

[402] Dobrynin, *In Confidence*, 365.

[403] Ibid., 366.

Chapter 5

The Role of Relationships

"He understood that a reputation for reliability is an important asset in foreign policy. Subtle and disciplined, warm in his demeanor while wary in his conduct, Dobrynin moved through the upper echelons of Washington with consummate skill."[1]

-Henry Kissinger

"To Henry, opponent, partner, friend."[2]

-Anatoly Dobrynin's inscription on a copy of his memoirs presented to Henry Kissinger

As the 1970s came to an end, the chances of a return to relaxing tensions appeared remote. No one seemed less likely to resume détente with the Soviet Union than Ronald Reagan, who was elected President of the United States in 1980. At his first presidential press conference Reagan called détente "a one-way street"[3] which he believed the Soviet Union had exploited to acquire a strategic and geopolitical advantage over the United States.

There was much to support this view. In addition to maintaining superiority in ICBMs and SLBMs (but not bombers) throughout the 1970s, in 1977 the Soviets had deployed new tactical nuclear missiles in Eastern Europe, the SS-20s.[4] These intermediate range ballistic missiles (IRBMs) with multiple warheads were capable of hitting Western European capitals, thus enhancing Moscow's regional nuclear advantage.[5] Additionally, the Soviets still held a considerable advantage in conventional forces on the continent. Left unchecked, such developments presented the theoretical possibility of the "Finlandization" of Europe, a

---

[1] Henry Kissinger, foreword to *Soviet-American Relations: The Détente Years, 1969-1972* (Washington, D.C.: United States Government Printing Office, 2007), x.

[2] Ibid.

[3] *Reagan*, produced by Adriana Bosch and Austin Hoyt, 253 min., WGBH Educational Foundation, 1998, DVD.

[4] Richard Burt, "The SS-20 and the Eurostrategic Balance," *The World Today* Vol. 33, No. 2 (Feb., 1977): 44.

[5] Ibid., 46, 48.

reference to Finland's perceived acquiescence to the neighboring Soviet Union on foreign policy in exchange for maintaining some measure of domestic sovereignty. If Europe as a whole felt compelled to take a similar path, it could split the North Atlantic Treaty Alliance (NATO) and leave the United States diplomatically isolated. Some Western European governments including Great Britain and West Germany were so concerned that they requested NATO to respond with its own intermediate range weapons. Despite fervent protests from the nuclear freeze movement, Reagan deployed intermediate range Tomahawk cruise missiles and Pershing II ballistic missiles in 1983.

In addition to the changes in the US-Soviet relationship, there were significant global developments as well. The "convergence theory" of liberal economist John Kenneth Galbraith postulated that multinational corporations in the West and communist state enterprises would become increasingly similar.[6] Such a view implied that communism remained a viable economic system and may have even been superior to capitalism in terms of managing industrial development.[7] Furthermore, around the world ten additional countries had adopted communist governments from 1975-1980. By the end of the decade Freedom House, a non- governmental organization (NGO) tracking the progress of democracy, noted that autocratic regimes of both the left and the right outnumbered democratic ones 2:1.[8] French scholar Jean-Francois Revel even warned of a "totalitarian temptation," arguing that many had come to believe dictatorships might be better suited to provide for people's needs than liberal democracies could.[9]

President Carter increased US defense spending as well as aid to the Mujahideen rebels fighting the Soviets in Afghanistan. However, Reagan's first term was marked by still greater increases in both as well as declarations of ideological warfare including describing the Soviet Union as an Evil Empire. Nevertheless, beginning in 1985 he and new Soviet General Secretary Mikhail Gorbachev held the first of four summits. Two years later they signed the Intermediate Range Nuclear Forces (INF) treaty

---

[6] Galen Mac Caba, review of *Strange Rebels: 1979 and the Birth of the 21st Century*, by Christian Caryl, in *National Review*, 17 June 2013, 53.

[7] Ibid., 53.

[8] Sandy Vogelgesang, "Diplomacy of Human Rights," *International Studies Quarterly* Vol. 23, No. 2, Special Issue on Human Rights (Jun. 1979): 218.

[9] Jean-Francois Revel, *The Totalitarian Temptation*, trans. David Hapgood (New York: Penguin Books, 1978), 9.

whereby both the United States and the Soviet Union agreed to eliminate an entire class of nuclear weapons. Additional negotiations commenced to drastically reduce – not simply limit – long-range strategic weapons, culminating in the 1991 Strategic Arms Reductions Treaty (START I) after Reagan left office. Unlike SALT, the START negotiations also included verification measures to ensure compliance with any agreement. US-Soviet relations continued to improve until the Soviet Union dissolved and the Cold War ended.

What happened? How did the United States and the Soviet Union go "[f]rom the second cold war to the second détente"[10] and ultimately to the end of the Cold War? It is one of the most intensely argued questions amongst historians of US-Soviet relations. Some scholars credited Mikhail Gorbachev and his policies of *glasnost* (openness) and *perestroika* (restructuring). They pointed to reforms granting Soviet citizens a greater role in their government as well as the release of Eastern Europe from Moscow's influence. However, they also acknowledged that Gorbachev lost control of the reform process, ultimately leading to the dissolution of the Union of Soviet Socialist Republics.[11] For many scholars on the left, Gorbachev was a great reformer and man of peace. However, observers on the right argued that Gorbachev's reforms were intended to salvage communism and find a way to make it more competitive with the West. He certainly did not plan to abolish the communist party and the Soviet Union itself. Furthermore, critics argued that Gorbachev's military response to independence movements in the Baltic States and elsewhere undermined the notion that he was simply a man dedicated to peacefully ending the Cold War.

Gorbachev's "new political thinking" about foreign policy was another proposed explanation for the Cold War's end. Advocates of this view contended that American fears of Soviet expansion had driven US-Soviet tensions ever since George Kennan's article "The Sources of Soviet Conduct," appeared in *Foreign Affairs* in 1947. Consequently, some cited

---

[10] Lawrence Freedman, *The Evolution of Nuclear Strategy*, third ed. (New York: Palgrave MacMillan, 2003), 378.

[11] For these arguments, see Robert G. Kaiser, *Why Gorbachev Happened – His Triumphs and Failure* (New York: Simon & Schuster, 1991); Robert V. Daniels, *The End of the Communist Revolution* (New York: Routledge, 1993); Raymond L. Garthoff, *The Great Transition: American-Soviet Relations and the End of the Cold War* (Washington, D.C.: The Brookings Institution, 1994); and Stephen F. Cohen, *Soviet Fates and Lost Alternatives - From Stalinism to the New Cold War* (New York: Columbia University Press, 2009).

Gorbachev's removal of ideological considerations from foreign policy such as support for the international "class struggle," as crucial to ending the East-West conflict.[12] This narrative may have appealed to those on the right who considered the Soviet Union to be motivated by Marxist-Leninist ideology to establishing global domination. However, for those on the left who believed such concerns to be misguided at best and paranoid at worst, this thesis was probably not as satisfying.

Others argued that none of Gorbachev's domestic and foreign policy reforms would have taken place without the hard-line policies of the first term Reagan administration from 1981-1984. They suggested that the Soviet Union only changed course from its aggressive posture after being confronted by counteroffensive measures taken by the United States including dramatic increases in defense spending and support for resistance movements in Eastern Europe and elsewhere. Furthermore, they pointed to Reagan's Strategic Defense Initiative (SDI) as presenting a technological challenge to the Soviet offensive nuclear arsenal which Moscow lacked the ability to duplicate. The cumulative effect of these policies was said to have forced Gorbachev to liberalize politically and economically, and ultimately led to the dissolution of the Soviet Union and the end of the Cold War.[13] However, some on the left argued that rather than bringing about or hastening the Cold War's end, Reagan's hard-line stance inflamed tensions and dragged the confrontation out longer than it needed to be. They also pointed to the enormous US

---

[12] For these arguments, see John Mueller, "What Was the Cold War About? Evidence from its Ending," *Political Science Quarterly* Vol. 119, No. 4 (Winter 2004/2005); Anatoli Cherniaev, "Gorbachev's Foreign Policy: The Concept," in *Turning Points in Ending the Cold War*, ed. Kiron K. Skinner (Stanford, CA: Hoover Institution Press, 2008); and Jack F. Matlock, Jr., "The End of Détente and the Reformulation of American Strategy: 1980-1983," in *Turning Points in Ending the Cold War*, ed. Kiron K. Skinner (Stanford, CA: Hoover Institution Press, 2008).

[13] For these arguments, see Richard Pipes, review of *The Great Transition: American-Soviet Relations and the End of the Cold War*, by Raymond L. Garthoff, in *Foreign Affairs* Vol. 74, No. 1 (Jan.-Feb., 1995); Andrew E. Busch, "Ronald Reagan and the Defeat of the Soviet Empire," *Presidential Studies Quarterly* Vol. 27, No. 3, The Presidency in the World (Summer, 1997); Robert G. Patman, "Reagan, Gorbachev and the Emergence of 'New Political Thinking,'" *Review of International Studies*, Vol. 25, No. 4 (Oct., 1999); Jack F. Matlock, Jr., "The End of Détente and the Reformulation of American Strategy: 1980-1983," in *Turning Points in Ending the Cold War*, ed. Kiron K. Skinner (Stanford, CA: Hoover Institution Press, 2008); and Kiron K. Skinner, "An Alternative Conception of Mutual Cooperation," in *Turning Points in Ending the Cold War*, ed. Kiron K. Skinner (Stanford, CA: Hoover Institution Press, 2008).

national debt resulting in part from Reagan's defense spending. On the other hand, many on the right pointed to several developments in the 1970s including the Soviet arms build-up, the use of Cuban surrogates in support of Marxist revolutions in the developing world, and the invasion of Afghanistan as evidence that US-Soviet relations were already at their nadir by the time Reagan came into office. Consequently, they argued that an aggressive response from the Americans was precisely what was required. Additionally, they contended that the installment of a reformer, Mikhail Gorbachev, as General Secretary of the Communist Party demonstrated that Reagan's approach did not result in an equally hard-line response from the Soviets.

Finally, several observers emphasized the role of personal relationships and trust which developed between key American and Soviet officials, somewhat reminiscent of that between Kissinger and Dobrynin via the backchannel over a decade before. They argued that despite Reagan's reputation as a hard-liner, he was genuinely interested in relaxing tensions. Gaddis claimed that Reagan shocked "his own hard-line supporters" when his foreign policy "turned out to be a more solidly based approach to détente than anything the Nixon, Ford, or Carter administrations had been able to accomplish."[14] While some in the administration like Secretary of Defense Caspar Weinberger viewed Reagan's arms build-up as an effort to "debilitate the other side," Gaddis explained that Reagan eventually sided with pragmatists like Secretary of State George Schultz in using it to compel the Soviets to negotiate.[15] Kiron K. Skinner, associate professor of International Relations at Carnegie Mellon University and research fellow at the Hoover Institution at Stanford University, argued that negotiations with Moscow were "as important as the military buildup," for Reagan's strategy.[16]

However, if US-Soviet relations were to improve it required a counterpart on the Soviet side. As Gaddis explained, only when Mikhail Gorbachev became General Secretary in 1985 did Reagan have a negotiating partner "imaginative" enough (or who lived long enough) with

---

[14] John Lewis Gaddis, *The United States and the End of the Cold War* (New York: Oxford University Press, 1992), 123.

[15] Ibid., 125.

[16] Kiron K. Skinner, "An Alternative Conception of Mutual Cooperation," in *Turning Points in Ending the Cold War*, ed. Kiron K. Skinner (Stanford, CA: Hoover Institution Press, 2008), 95.

whom to do business.[17] Jack F. Matlock, Jr., Reagan's ambassador to Moscow, agreed and explained that beginning in 1983 the Reagan administration "tried to establish a pattern of discussing new proposals with the Soviet Communist Party leader in private before making them public."[18] This included the use of letters (many hand-written by Reagan personally) as well as meetings between diplomats.[19] However, "it took two or three years to catch on and be reciprocated,"[20] suggesting that real progress did not commence until Gorbachev arrived on the scene.

By the time of the first Reagan-Gorbachev summit in 1985 at Geneva, Gorbachev's chief foreign policy advisor Anatoli Cherniaev observed "some sort of human rapport between the two leaders that gave hope for change."[21] Cherniaev added that after Reagan's positive reaction to Gorbachev's 1986 proposal at Reykjavik to eliminate half of all strategic nuclear weapons, "Mutual trust between the two leaders was another touchstone of the new political thinking that was crucial in bringing the cold war to an end."[22] Ultimately, both Reagan and Gorbachev stopped viewing the Cold War as a zero-sum game or in the words of Arthur M. Schlesinger, Jr. as if "a gain for one side was by definition a defeat for the other."[23] The old outlook had led not to "negotiation," but rather "to a demand for capitulation," said Schlesinger.[24]

However, the change in approach was not limited to the two men at the top. Citing the memoirs of numerous Soviet officials as well as archival documents, William D. Jackson argued "the interest displayed by the second-term Reagan administration in improving relations with Moscow and *the personal trust* [italics mine] that gradually developed in

---

[17] Gaddis, *The United States and the End of the Cold War*, 126.

[18] Jack F. Matlock, Jr., "Empathy in International Relations: A Commentary," *Journal of Cold War Studies* Vol. 12, No. 2 (Spring 2010): 90.

[19] Ibid.

[20] Ibid.

[21] Anatoli Cherniaev, "Gorbachev's Foreign Policy: The Concept," in *Turning Points in Ending the Cold War*, ed. Kiron K. Skinner (Stanford, CA: Hoover Institution Press, 2008), 117.

[22] Ibid., 124.

[23] Arthur M. Schlesinger, Jr. "Some Lessons from the Cold War," in *The Cold War*, ed. Klaus Larres and Anne Lane (Malden, Massachusetts: Blackwell Publishers, Inc., 2001), 238.

[24] Ibid.

high-level contacts between Soviet and U.S. officials" altered U.S.-Soviet relations and led to the end of the Cold War.[25]

Like American and Soviet officials during the Reagan-Gorbachev era, the telephone transcripts show that Kissinger and Dobrynin developed a relationship while developing détente. The backchannel had four qualities which helped to facilitate this: privacy, durability, ease and frequency of communication, and the personalities of its participants.

As the scholarly literature on back channels has argued, privacy allows representatives from opposing sides to begin talks when more strident voices on both ends may be opposed to any form of negotiations. This was certainly true during the détente era as relaxing US-Soviet tensions faced opposition from hard-liners in Moscow and both liberals and conservatives in Washington. Additionally, Kissinger and Dobrynin worked jointly to keep the substance of their face-to-face meetings and telephone calls secret, creating a bond while establishing trust.

Second, the Kissinger-Dobrynin backchannel had durability. For eight years, they were the main point of contact for each other when addressing US-Soviet relations. While previous back channels had dealt with a specific issue or emergency, as with the Cuban Missile Crisis in 1962, the Kissinger-Dobrynin backchannel was a permanent link between the White House and the Kremlin for all aspects of US-Soviet diplomacy. It lasted through a presidential election in 1972, Kissinger's appointment as Secretary of State in 1973, the Watergate scandal and Nixon's subsequent resignation in 1974, and even when Kissinger was stripped of his National Security Advisor duties by President Ford in 1975.

Third, the structure of the backchannel provided an ease and frequency of communication unlike any other channel. Since Dobrynin was stationed at the Soviet embassy in Washington, he could conveniently meet with Kissinger in the Map Room of the White House. Initially they met on a weekly basis, however the frequency increased as time went on. Furthermore, the ease of access provided by the hotline from Dobrynin's office at the Soviet embassy to Kissinger's office in the White House probably encouraged more frequent communication than would have taken place otherwise.

Finally, the backchannel was effective due to the personal chemistry of its participants. This was its most intangible quality, but nevertheless a significant one. To put it simply, Kissinger and Dobrynin

---

[25] William D. Jackson, "Soviet Reassessment of Ronald Reagan, 1985-88," *Political Science Quarterly*, Vol. 113, No. 4 (Winter, 1998-1999): 618.

"hit it off." Dobrynin in particular appreciated their shared sense of humor, which he said "helps to reach the heart as well as the mind of your partner."[26] Indeed, their banter was often comical, occasionally bordering on bawdy. Alistair Horne described some of their conversations as more typical of "old college roommates" rather than representatives of the superpowers.[27]

Through a common purpose and shared experience, Kissinger and Dobrynin built a relationship and established empathy. However, empathy does not equal sympathy. Ralph K. White, a political scientist and psychologist at George Washington University, wrote that empathy is "'simply understanding the thoughts and feelings of others. It is distinguished from sympathy, which is defined as feeling with others – as being in agreement with them.'"[28] Consequently, "'even when a conflict is so intense that sympathy is out of the question,'" empathy is nevertheless possible.[29]

Recent scholarship about the failure of détente focused on the issue of empathy. As James G. Blight and Janet M. Lang explained, "empathy is a central concept in such fields as anthropology (especially ethnography), clinical psychology, and conflict resolution, among others," but not in Cold War history.[30] Nevertheless, they contended that the initial March 1977 arms control meeting in Moscow between the new Carter administration and the Kremlin was a turning point in US-Soviet relations due to a lack of empathy on both sides. According to Blight and Lang, both the Americans and the Soviets agreed that this was the beginning of the mistrust which eventually ended détente.[31]

---

[26] Anatoly Dobrynin, *In Confidence – Moscow's Ambassador to Six Cold War Presidents (1962-1986)* (New York: Times Books, 1995), 206.

[27] Alistair Horne, *Kissinger – 1973, The Crucial Year* (New York: Simon & Schuster, 2009), 139, 140.

[28] Ralph K. White, *Fearful Warriors: A Psychological Profile of U.S.-Soviet Relations* (New York: Freed Press, 1984), 160; cited in James G. Blight and Janet M. Lang, "Forum: When Empathy Failed – Using Critical Oral History to Reassess the Collapse of U.S. Soviet Détente in the Carter-Brezhnev Years," *Journal of Cold War Studies* Vol. 12, No. 2 (Spring 2010): 39.

[29] Ibid.

[30] James G. Blight and Janet M. Lang, "Forum: When Empathy Failed – Using Critical Oral History to Reassess the Collapse of U.S. Soviet Détente in the Carter-Brezhnev Years," *Journal of Cold War Studies* Vol. 12, No. 2 (Spring 2010): 41.

[31] Ibid., 43.

The authors examined the published proceedings of the Carter-Brezhnev Project, part of the Watson Institute for International Studies at Brown University. A May, 1994, conference in Musgrove, Georgia entitled "SALT II and the Growth of Mistrust," featured many of the most significant players from 1977 including President Carter's Secretary of State Cyrus Vance, National Security Advisor Zbigniew Brzezinski, Dobrynin, and Russian translator Viktor Sukhodrev. The goals of the conference were to identify mistakes, look for missed opportunities, and draw lessons from the 1977 Moscow summit.[32] Blight and Lang explained that by using critical oral history, a process "combining, in structured conferences, decision-makers, scholars, and declassified documents (which provide added accuracy and authenticity to the conversation)," the participants were able to establish empathy and "begin to develop the capacity to see pivotal events more or less the way their former adversaries saw them at the time."[33] Blight and Lang explained that this method "often yields rich and surprising insights into what it was really like for decision-makers, then and there, thus yielding more accurate analyses and applicable lessons for decision-making, here and now."[34] The inclusion of testimony from both sides, plus questions from scholars "armed with declassified documents," helps to provide greater certainty of what happened, as much as this is possible in the search for historical truth.[35]

The 1994 conference revealed that the Soviets had taken offense at the 1977 summit when the Americans proposed a much more radical arms limitation agreement than the one agreed upon between President Ford and General Secretary Brezhnev at Vladivostok in 1974.[36] The Soviets viewed this as a unilateral change, while the Americans were offended at the lack of any counterproposal.[37] The use of critical oral history enabled both sides to understand what the other had thought at the time. Blight and Lang concluded that the history of détente could have been more successful if only the two sides had been able to see the other's point of view.[38]

---

[32] Ibid., 32.

[33] Ibid., 34, 38, 40.

[34] Ibid., 34.

[35] Ibid., 35, 38.

[36] Ibid., 48.

[37] Ibid., 48, 67, 68.

[38] Ibid., 74.

While at the conference Dobrynin reflected on his experience negotiating in the backchannel. He explained that it was not a panacea for successful diplomacy, but it did allow both sides to make proposals in an informal way, and thereby gauge the other's reaction as well as the chances for success:

> I don't say that it is something of overriding importance, but it has some importance. Specifically in one sense: it gives you a chance to explain things. It helps provide preliminary explanation of the position of the other country. It's simple. It doesn't always matter who the channel is; things are decided by the president. But the Backchannel helps elaborate on your thinking a bit. Not always.[39]

However, without this line of communication, Dobrynin claimed that the Soviets were unsure of what the Carter administration wanted to do and where they wanted to take the relationship:

> There was one situation when the secretary of state [Cyrus Vance] brought one proposal-drastic reductions-and someone else brought another one. And someone would raise human rights. It was difficult to know how to deal with this [the Carter] administration at all.[40]

In short, Dobrynin explained that the backchannel allowed for elaboration and clarification of positions. "It is important not just to have people come with very big proposals, accompanied by some other things which were not acceptable. You need contacts to explain things," he added.[41] Although Dobrynin had attempted to initiate backchannel negotiations with Carter's National Security Advisor Zbigniew Brzezinski, the new

---

[39] The Carter-Brezhnev Project, "SALT II and the Growth of Mistrust," Thomas J. Watson Institute for International Studies (Brown University, 1994), 60. Available at www.gwu.edu/~nsarchiv/nukevault/ebb285/doc03.pdf.
[40] Ibid.
[41] Ibid.

president opposed "secret diplomacy" and insisted that all business be done with the State Department and its Secretary Cyrus Vance.[42]

It is apparent that from Dobrynin's point of view, the American-Soviet relationship no longer possessed empathy by the time of the March, 1977 meeting. The Americans did not understand that the Soviets felt they had neither been consulted nor respected when Vance made a new arms control offer. The agenda and the proposals stemming from that agenda had been created by the US.[43] As Dobrynin put it, "If we want to understand the fight we had for years with your administration, we have to look at your agenda. Wrongly or rightly, that is how we saw things. That's why we were so angry, and didn't even want to discuss your proposals."[44]

However, there was plenty of blame to go around. At the same 1994 conference, former Secretary of State Cyrus Vance expressed his frustration at the unequivocal Soviet rejection of the American proposal in 1977:

> The problem that really arose, it seems to me, was that when we put our proposals on the table, nobody would listen to them, and contrary to usual practice, nobody said, 'Well, let's sit down and talk about that and see if we can find a way to get around this thing.' We got a wet rag in the face, and were told to go home.[45]

President Carter's stated goal was to eventually rid the world of all nuclear weapons.[46] Representatives of his administration believed that they had made an honest attempt at a first step towards that objective. It was then immediately rejected. Vance called the rejection a crucial "tactical mistake" and claimed that several years later Soviet Foreign Minister Andrei Gromyko agreed with him.[47]

As Blight and Lang explained, even though nuclear arms control "was by far the top priority on their mutual agenda," both sides came away

---

[42] Vladislav Zubok, *A Failed Empire – The Soviet Union in the Cold War from Stalin to Gorbachev* (Chapel Hill: The University of North Carolina Press, 2007), 255.
[43] Carter-Brezhnev Project, 60-61.
[44] Ibid., 61.
[45] Ibid., 62.
[46] Jimmy Carter, *Keeping Faith* (New York: Bantam Books, 1982), 215.
[47] Carter-Brezhnev Project, 62.

from the March, 1977 summit believing that the other was "not serious."[48] Regardless of who was to blame, it is extremely difficult to imagine such a situation occurring in the days of reliance on the backchannel. The channel was more than a preliminary means of communication. It facilitated understanding and compromise. Any new proposal for a radical reduction in nuclear arms would have first been discussed between Kissinger and Dobrynin before either side presented it at a formal summit meeting. One of the things which might have been discovered was Brezhnev's strong emotional attachment to the November, 1974, Vladivostok Accords. The Soviet General Secretary believed that the difficulties he encountered while getting the Politburo to accept this agreement contributed to the stroke he suffered shortly after Vladivostok.[49] In short, Brezhnev thought he had sacrificed his health to forge the deal.[50] This kind of information could have been shared privately in the backchannel before taking any new proposal to either side's leadership.

To be very clear, the emphasis on the relationship between Kissinger and Dobrynin is not to make a value judgment on them, their politics, or their successors. Nor is it an attempt to blame the collapse of détente entirely on the end of the Kissinger-Dobrynin backchannel. Rather, it is intended to offer a possible explanation for the relative success of détente during its early years in spite of the strongly conflicting American and Soviet ideologies.

Even if one does accept the value of relationships and the empathy it helps to create, it raises another question. Does this type of interpretive tool cause the historian to focus too heavily on a few individuals, thereby missing the larger picture? This is a possible danger. After all, not every diplomatic success or failure can be attributed to the actions of individuals. Sometimes, there is simply no common ground between the various interests of states.

Nevertheless, Deborah Welch Larson applied social psychology to make the case that sometimes countries fail to reach agreements "even when they have compatible preferences."[51] This occurs "because policy-makers make incorrect inferences about the opponent's motives and

---

[48] Blight and Lang, 67.

[49] Ibid., 69.

[50] Ibid.

[51] Deborah Welch Larson, "Trust and Opportunities in International Relations," *Political Psychology* Vol. 18, No. 3 (Sep., 1997): 701.

intentions."[52] However, states and diplomats who establish a relationship over an extended period of time may learn to cooperate despite great differences, because they can empathize with each other's efforts and recognize the potential benefits which can accrue to both sides from sticking things out.[53]

Differences between state systems can impede this process. For example, a non-democratic nation may "inspire distrust of their motives," but a democratic state can "elicit doubts of their resolution."[54] In a country with a democratic form of government, there is always the possibility of new leadership coming to power at the next election and hence a change in policy.[55] Therefore, the transition from the Nixon/Ford/Kissinger Era to the Carter administration may have presented an obstacle to détente not for any partisan, personal, or policy reasons, but simply because it represented a break from the past where a degree of trust had been established, particularly through the Kissinger-Dobrynin backchannel. On the other hand, in a long-term relationship (diplomatically speaking) such as the one which occurred between Kissinger and Dobrynin from 1969-1977, both sides can develop the belief that the other means well, and even "discount or overlook the other state's misdeeds or lies because such evidence is inconsistent with [their] image of the state as friendly."[56]

According to Larson, one way a nation can establish trust is though "a conciliatory gesture" which does not appear to benefit it in any way, and may even be potentially detrimental.[57] Such an action can enhance a nation's credibility if it is "noncontingent," "irrevocable," and increases its "vulnerability."[58]

The early détente period provided an apt example of such a "conciliatory gesture." Human rights were not on Moscow's agenda, and the specific issue of emigration from the Soviet Union arguably threatened Soviet security with the possibility that the government could lose control over its population. Furthermore, the notion that Soviet citizens might want to leave their country was inherently embarrassing for Moscow.

---

[52] Ibid.

[53] Ibid., 707.

[54] Ibid., 713.

[55] Ibid.

[56] Ibid., 715.

[57] Ibid., 721.

[58] Ibid.

Nevertheless, through the Kissinger-Dobrynin channel and without a great deal of attention, beginning around 1970 the Soviets gradually increased the number of exit visas granted to Soviet Jews. Meanwhile, the Americans reciprocated by keeping discussions of Jewish emigration in the backchannel and not using the issue for propaganda purposes. These early actions undoubtedly contributed to an improved climate in Soviet-American relations and helped lead to some of the greatest achievements of the détente period.

For eight years, Kissinger and Dobrynin discussed numerous issues as they built détente. The subjects ranged from arms control to human rights to foreign interventions in the developing world. With each successive crisis they faced, these representatives of the two superpowers built a relationship based upon a mutual commitment to relaxing tensions and avoiding nuclear war. A common purpose and shared experience created empathy and enabled both to navigate tumultuous diplomatic waters. After all, they were in it *together*. It may not even be an exaggeration to say they became friends – they clearly became *friendly*.

When détente ended along with the 1970s, it was because of fundamental ideological differences between the United States and the Soviet Union about relationships between states and the relationship between a state and its people. These differences had long been a part of US-Soviet relations, but détente's early successes had made them seem less significant. Until the American and Soviet leadership dealt with the root causes of the Cold War (this task was ultimately left to Reagan and Gorbachev in the 1980s) there would always be a limit to what could be accomplished diplomatically. This demonstrates the challenge faced by Kissinger and Dobrynin. In this light, the successes of their "special relationship" are all the more noteworthy and provide a case study of the potential for back channels to bring about resolutions in international crises.

Bibliography

Articles

Ambrose, Stephen E. "The Christmas Bombing." In *The Cold War – A Military History*, ed. Robert Cowley, 397-416. New York: Random House, 2005.

Anderson, Richard D. Jr., Margaret G. Hermann and Charles Hermann. "Explaining Self-Defeating Foreign Policy Decisions: Interpreting Soviet Arms for Egypt in 1973 through Process or Domestic Bargaining Models?" *The American Political Science Review* Vol. 86, No. 3 (Sep., 1992): 759-766.

Betts, Richard K. "The Lost Logic of Deterrence." *Foreign Affairs* Vol. 92, No. 2 (March/April, 2013): 87-99.

Bienen, Henry. "Perspectives on Soviet Intervention in Africa." *Political Science Quarterly* Vol. 95, No. 1 (Spring, 1980): 29-42.

Blight, James G. and Janet M. Lang. "Forum: When Empathy Failed – Using Critical Oral History to Reassess the Collapse of U.S. Soviet Détente in the Carter-Brezhnev Years." *Journal of Cold War Studies* Vol. 12, No. 2 (Spring 2010): 29-74.

Brennan, Edward J. "East-West Relations: The Role of Ideology." *Irish Studies in International Affairs* Vol. 2, No. 1 (1985): 51-101.

Brumberg, Abraham. "The Rise of Dissent in the U.S.S.R." In *In Quest of Justice – Protest and Dissent in the Soviet Union Today*, ed. Abraham Brumberg, 3-15. New York: Praeger Publishers, 1970.

Burr, William. "Omissions." Available on the National Security Archive website at: http://www.gwu.edu/~nsarchiv/nsa/publication/DOC_readers/kissinger/ommission.htm.

Burt, Richard. "The SS-20 and the Eurostrategic Balance." *The World Today* Vol. 33, No. 2 (Feb., 1977): 43-51.

189

Busch, Andrew E. "Ronald Reagan and the Defeat of the Soviet Empire." *Presidential Studies Quarterly* Vol. 27, No. 3, The Presidency in the World (Summer, 1997): 451-466.

Chambers, John Whiteclay II, ed. *The Oxford Companion to American Military History*. New York: Oxford University Press, 1999.   S.v. "Middle East, U.S. Military Involvement In The," by Douglas Little.

Chambers, John Whiteclay II, ed. *The Oxford Companion to American Military History*. New York: Oxford University Press, 1999. S.v. "SALT Treaties," by Raymond Garthoff.

Chambers, John Whiteclay II, ed. *The Oxford Companion to American Military History* New York: Oxford University Press, 1999.   S.v. "Vietnam War (1960-1975): Causes," by Andrew J. Rotter.

Chambers, John Whiteclay II, ed. *The Oxford Companion to American Military History* New York: Oxford University Press, 1999.   S.v. "Vietnam War (1960-1975): Military and Diplomatic Course," by   David L. Anderson.

Cherniaev, Anatoli. "Gorbachev's Foreign Policy: The Concept."   In *Turning Points in Ending the Cold War*. ed. Kiron K. Skinner, 111-140. Stanford, CA: Hoover Institution Press, 2008.

D'Souza, Dinesh. "How Reagan Won the Cold War." *National   Review*, 24 November 1997, 39.

Edwards, Geoffrey. "Human Rights and Basket III Issues: Areas of Change and Continuity." *International Affairs* Vol. 61, No. 4 (Autumn 1985): 631-642.

Hawkesworth, Mary. "Ideological Immunity: The Soviet Response to Human Rights Criticism." *Universal Human Rights* Vol. 2, No. 1 (Jan.-Mar., 1980): 67-84.

Holmes, Richard, ed. *The Oxford Companion to   Military   History*. Oxford: Oxford University Press, 2001. S.v. "Strategic   Arms Limitation/Strategic Arms Reduction Talks," by Sebastian Roberts.

Husband, William B. "Soviet Perceptions of U.S. 'Positions-of-Strength' Diplomacy in the 1970s." *World Politics* Vol. 31, No. 4, (Jul., 1979): 495-517.

Jackson, William D. "Soviet Reassessment of Ronald Reagan, 1985-88." *Political Science Quarterly* Vol. 113, No. 4 (Winter, 1998-1999): 617-644.

Jones, Matthew. "Between the Bear and the Dragon: Nixon, Kissinger and U.S. Foreign Policy in the Era of Détente." *English Historical Review* Vol. CXXIII, No. 504 (Oct., 2008): 1272-1283.

Kotsonis, Yonni. "A European Experience: Human Rights and Citizenship in Revolutionary Russia." In *Human Rights and Revolutions*, eds. Jeffrey N. Wasserstrom, Lynn Hunt, and Marilyn B. Young, 99-110. Lanham, Maryland: Rowman & Littlefield Publishers, Inc., 2000.

Larson, Deborah Welch. "Trust and Missed Opportunities in International Relations." *Political Psychology* Vol. 18, No. 3 (Sep., 1997): 701-734.

Lemke, Douglas and Suzanne Werner. "Power Parity, Commitment to Change, and War." *International Studies Quarterly* Vol. 40, No. 2 (Jun., 1996): 235-260.

Lider, Julian. "The Correlation of World Forces: The Soviet Concept." *Journal of Peace Research* Vol. 17, No. 2, (1980): 151-171.

Mac Caba, Galen. Review of *Strange Rebels: 1979 and the Birth of the 21st Century*, by Christian Caryl. In *National Review*, 17 June 2013, 53.

Margolin, Jean-Louis. "Vietnam and Laos: The Impasse of War Communism." In *The Black Book of Communism*, ed. Stephane Courtois, et. al., 565-576. Translated by Jonathan Murphy and Mark Kramer. Cambridge, Massachusetts: Harvard University Press, 1999.

Matlock, Jack F. Jr. "The End of Détente and the Reformulation of American Strategy: 1980-1983." In *Turning Points in Ending the Cold War*, ed. Kiron K. Skinner, 11-39. Stanford, CA: Hoover Institution Press, 2008.

Mirski, Georgi I. "Soviet-American Relations in the Third World." In *Turning Points in Ending the Cold War*, ed. Kiron K. Skinner, 149-181. Stanford, CA: Hoover Institution Press, 2008.

Montgomery, Bruce P. "'*Source Material*': Sequestered from the Court of History: The Kissinger Transcripts." *Presidential Studies Quarterly* Vol. 34, No. 4 (Dec., 2004): 867-890.

Mueller, John. "What Was the Cold War About? Evidence from Its Ending." *Political Science Quarterly* Vol. 119, No. 4 (Winter, 2004/2005): 609-631.

Noer, Thomas J. "International Credibility and Political Survival: The Ford Administration's Intervention in Angola." *Presidential Studies Quarterly* Vol. 23, No. 4, The Managerial, Political and Spiritual Presidencies (Fall, 1993): 771-785.

O'Dochartaigh, Niall. "Together in the middle: Back-channel negotiation in the Irish peace process." *Journal of Peace Research* Vol. 48, No. 6 (November 2011): 767-780.

Parker, F. Charles. "The Third World in Soviet Strategy, 1945-1980." *Asian Affairs* Vol. 7, No. 6, (Jul.-Aug., 1980): 341-369.

Patman, Robert G. "Reagan, Gorbachev and the Emergence of 'New Political Thinking.'" *Review of International Studies* Vol. 25, No. 4, (Oct., 1999): 577-601.

Pipes, Richard. Review of *The Great Transition: American-Soviet Relations and the End of the Cold War*, by Raymond L. Garthoff. In *Foreign Affairs* Vol. 74, No. 1 (Jan.-Feb., 1995): 154-160.

Richter, James. "Perpetuating the Cold War: Domestic Sources of International Patterns of Behavior." *Political Science Quarterly* Vol. 107, No. 2 (Summer, 1992): 271-301.

Safire, William. "The Suspicious 17; Essay." *New York Times*, 9 August 1973.

Santamaria, Yves. "Afrocommunism: Ethiopia, Angola, and Mozambique." In *The Black Book of Communism*, ed. Stephane Courtois, et. al., 683-704. Translated by Jonathan Murphy and Mark Kramer. Cambridge, Massachusetts: Harvard University Press, 1999.

Schlesinger, Arthur M. Jr. "Some Lessons from the Cold War." In *The Cold War*, ed. Klaus Larres and Anne Lane, 238. Malden, Massachusetts: Blackwell Publishers, Inc., 2001.

Skinner, Kiron K. "An Alternative Conception of Mutual Cooperation." In *Turning Points in Ending the Cold War*, ed. Kiron K. Skinner, 93-110. Stanford, CA: Hoover Institution Press, 2008.

Tucker, Nancy Bernkopf. "China as a Factor in the Collapse of the Soviet Empire." *Political Science Quarterly* Vol. 110, No. 4 (Winter, 1995-1996): 501-518.

Vogelgesang, Sandy. "Diplomacy of Human Rights." *International Studies Quarterly* Vol. 23, No. 2, Special Issue on Human Rights: International Perspectives, (Jun., 1979): 216-245.

Werth, Nicholas. "A State Against Its People: Violence, Repression, and Terror in the Soviet Union." In *The Black Book of Communism*, ed. Stephane Courtois, et. al., 33-268. Translated by Jonathan Murphy and Mark Kramer. Cambridge, Massachusetts: Harvard University Press, 1999.

Zagare, Frank. "Reconciling Rationality with Deterrence: A Re-examination of the Logical Foundations of Deterrence Theory." *Journal of Theoretical Politics* Vol. 16, No. 2 (2004): 107-141.

Books
Aitken, Jonathan. *Nixon – A Life*. Washington, D.C.: Regnery Publishing, Inc., 1993.

Alexander, Bevin. *How America Got It Right – The U.S. March to Military and Political Supremacy*. New York: Crown Forum, 2005.

Andrew, Christopher and Vasili Mitrokhin. *The World Was Going Our Way – The KGB and the Battle for the Third World*. New York: Basic Books, 2005.

Applebaum, Anne. *Gulag – A History*. New York: Doubleday, 2003.

Arbatov, Georgi. *The System – An Insider's Life in Soviet Politics*. New York: Random House, Inc., 1992.

Beichman, Arnold. *The Long Pretense*. New Brunswick: Transaction Publishers, 1991.

Beichman, Arnold and Mikhail S. Bernstam. *Andropov – New Challenge to the West*. New York: Stein and Day, 1983.

Bickerton, Ian J. and Carla L. Klausner. *A Concise History of the Arab-Israeli Conflict*. Third ed. Upper Saddle River, New Jersey: Prentice Hall, 1998.

Buckley, William F., Jr. *The Fall of the Berlin Wall*. Hoboken, New Jersey: John Wiley & Sons, Inc., 2004.

Burr, William. *The Kissinger Transcripts: The Top Secret Talks with Beijing and Moscow*. New York: The New Press, 1998.

Clodfelter, Mark. *The Limits of Airpower – The American Bombing of North Vietnam*. New York: The Free Press, 1989.

Cohen, Stephen F. *Soviet Fates and Lost Alternatives – From Stalinism to the New Cold War*. New York: Columbia University Press, 2009.

Crocker III, H.W. *Don't Tread on Me – A 400-Year History of America at War, from Indian Fighting to Terrorist Hunting*. New York: Crown Forum, 2006.

Crozier, Brian. *The Rise and Fall of the Soviet Empire*. Rocklin, CA: Prima Publishing, 1999.

Dallek, Robert. *Nixon and Kissinger: Partners in Power*. New York: HarperCollins, 2007.

Daniels, Robert V. *The End of the Communist Revolution*. New York: Routledge, 1993.

Freedman, Lawrence. *The Evolution of Nuclear Strategy*. Third ed. New York: Palgrave Publishers Ltd., 2003.

Gaddis, John Lewis. *The Cold War – A New History*. New York: The Penguin Press, 2005.

Gaddis, John Lewis. *The United States and the End of the Cold War*. New York: Oxford University Press, 1992.

Gaddis, John Lewis. *We Now Know – Rethinking Cold War History*. New York: Oxford University Press, 1997.

Garthoff, Raymond L. *Détente and Confrontation: American-Soviet Relations from Nixon to Reagan*. Washington, D.C.: Brookings Institution, 1985.

Garthoff, Raymond L. *The Great Transition: American-Soviet Relations and the End of the Cold War*. Washington, D.C.: Brookings Institution, 1994.

Gates, Robert M. *From the Shadows – The Ultimate Insider's Story of Five Presidents and How They Won the Cold War*. New York: Simon & Schuster, 1996.

Gelman, Harry. *The Brezhnev Politburo and the Decline of Détente*. Ithaca: Cornell University Press, 1984.

Hayward, Stephen F. *The Age of Reagan – The Fall of the Old Liberal Order, 1964-1980*. Roseville, CA: Prima Publishing, 2001.

Hobsbawm, Eric. *The Age of Extremes*. New York: Pantheon Books, 1994.

Horne, Alistair. *Kissinger – 1973, The Crucial Year*. New York: Simon & Schuster, 2009.

Isaacson, Walter. *Kissinger – A Biography*. New York: Simon & Schuster, 1992.

Johnson, Paul. *Modern Times*. New York: HarperCollins Publishers, 1991.

Kaiser, Robert G. *Why Gorbachev Happened – His Triumphs and Failure*. New York: Simon & Schuster, 1991.

Lauren, Paul Gordon. *The Evolution of International Human Rights*. Philadelphia: University of Pennsylvania Press. 2003.

Leffler, Melvyn P. *For the Soul of Mankind – The United States, the Soviet Union, and the Cold War*. New York: Hill and Wang, 2007.

Lind, Michael. *Vietnam: The Necessary War*. New York: The Free Press, 1999.

Maresca, John J. *To Helsinki*. Durham, North Carolina: Duke University Press. 1985.

Marx, Karl and Friedrich Engels. *The Communist Manifesto*. New York: Simon & Schuster Inc., 1964.

Matusow, Allen J. *The Unraveling of America – A History of Liberalism in the 1960s*. New York: Harper & Row, 1984.

Mearsheimer, John J. *The Tragedy of Great Power Politics*. New York: W. W. Norton and Company, 2001.

Medvedev, Zhores. *Andropov*. New York: W.W. Norton & Company, 1983.

Melanson, Richard A. *American Foreign Policy Since the Vietnam War – The Search for Consensus from Nixon to Clinton*. Armonk, New York: M.E. Sharpe, 1996.

Mieczkowski, Yanek. *Gerald Ford and the Challenges of the 1970s.* Lexington: The University Press of Kentucky, 2005.

Morgan, Iwan W. *Beyond the Liberal Consensus – A Political History of the United States Since 1965.* New York: St. Martin's Press, 1993.

Morris, Benny. *Righteous Victims – A History of the Zionist-Arab Conflict, 1881-2001.* New York: Vintage Books, 2001.

Morris, James M. *America's Armed Forces – A History.* Englewood Cliffs, New Jersey: Prentice Hall, 1991.

Nelson, Keith L. *The Making of Détente – Soviet-American Relations in the Shadow of Vietnam.* Baltimore: Johns Hopkins University Press, 1995.

Organski, A.F.K. and Jacek Kugler. *The War Ledger.* Chicago: University of Chicago Press, 1980.

O'Toole, G.J.A. *Honorable Treachery – A History of U.S. Intelligence, Espionage, and Covert Action from the American Revolution to the CIA.* New York: The Atlantic Monthly Press, 1991.

Perry, Glenn E. *The Middle East – Fourteen Islamic Centuries.* Third ed. Upper Saddle River, New Jersey: Prentice Hall, 1997.

Petroff, Serge. *The Red Eminence – A Biography of Mikhail A. Suslov.* Clifton, New Jersey: The Kingston Press, Inc., 1988.

Podhoretz, Norman. *The Present Danger.* New York: Simon & Schuster, 1980.

Powers, Richard Gid. *Not Without Honor – The History of American Anti-Communism.* New Haven: Yale University Press, 1998.

Pryce-Jones, David. *The Strange Death of the Soviet Empire.* New York: Henry Holt and Company, 1995.

Reed, Thomas C. *At the Abyss – An Insider's History of the Cold War*. New York: Ballantine Books, 2004.

Revel, Jean-Francois. *The Totalitarian Temptation*. Translated by David Hapgood. New York: Penguin Books, 1978.

Sharansky, Natan with Ron Dermer. *The Case for Democracy – the Power of Freedom to Overcome Tyranny and Terror*. New York: Public Affairs, 2004.

Simes, Dimitri K. *Détente and Conflict: Soviet Foreign Policy, 1972-1977*. The Center for Strategic and International Studies. Georgetown University, Washington, D.C. Beverly Hills: Sage Publications, 1977.

Stevenson, Richard W. *The Rise and Fall of Détente – Relaxation of Tension in US-Soviet Relations, 1953-84*. Urbana and Chicago: University of Illinois Press, 1985.

Strayer, Robert. *Why Did the Soviet Union Collapse?* Armonk, New York: M.E. Sharpe, 1998.

Tammen Ronald L, et al. *Power Transitions – Strategies for the 21st Century*. New York: Chatham House Publishers, 2000.

Thornton, Richard C. *The Nixon-Kissinger Years – The Reshaping of American Foreign Policy*. 2nd ed. St. Paul, Minnesota: Paragon House, 2001.

Tompson, William. *The Soviet Union under Brezhnev*. London: Pearson Education Limited, 2003.

Ulam, Adam. *Dangerous Relations – The Soviet Union in World Politics, 1970-1982*. New York: Oxford University Press, 1983.

Volkogonov, Dmitri. *Autopsy for an Empire*. Translated by Harold Shukman. New York: The Free Press, 1998.

Waltz, Kenneth N. *Theory of International Politics*. New York: McGraw- Hill, Inc. 1979

Wanis-St. John. *Back Channel Negotiation: Secrecy in the Middle East Peace Process*. Syracuse, NY: Syracuse University Press, 2010.

Weissmann, Mikael. *The East Asian Peace: Conflict Prevention and Informal Peacebuilding*. Basingstoke: Palgrave Macmillan, 2012.

Westad, Odd Arne. *The Global Cold War – Third World Interventions and the Making of Our Times*. New York: Cambridge University Press, 2007.

Winik, Jay. *On the Brink – The Dramatic, Behind-the-Scenes Saga of the Reagan Era and the Men and Women Who Won the Cold War*. New York: Simon & Schuster, 1996.

Zubok, Vladislav M. *A Failed Empire – The Soviet Union in the Cold War from Stalin to Gorbachev*. Chapel Hill: The University of North Carolina Press, 2007.

Conference Reports
The Carter-Brezhnev Project. "SALT II and the Growth of Mistrust." Watson Institute for International Studies, Brown University, 1994. Available at http://www.gwu.edu/~nsarchiv/nukevault/ebb285/doc03.pdf and http://www.gwu.edu/~nsarchiv/nsaebb/nsaebb313/doc14.pdf.

Government Documents and Publications
Conference on Security and Co-operation in Europe. *Final Act*. August 1, 1975.

The Henry A. Kissinger Telephone Conversation Transcripts (Telcons). [Anatoli Dobrynin File. Boxes 27 and 28.] Richard Nixon Presidential Library and Museum, Yorba Linda, California. National Archives and Records Administration.

"Kissinger Transcripts." United States Department of State. Available at http://foia.state.gov/SearchColls/CollsSearch.asp.

Nixon Presidential Materials Staff. "The Henry A. Kissinger Telephone Conversation Transcripts (Telcons)." National Archives and Records Administration, 2004.

Susser, Mark J. Preface to *Soviet-American Relations: The Détente Years, 1969-1972*. Washington, D.C.: United States Government Printing Office, 2007.

The United States Helsinki Watch Committee. *Ten Years Later – Violations of the Helsinki Accords*. New York and Washington, D.C. 1985.

The White House. "Jackson-Vanik and Russia Fact Sheet." Available at www.whitehouse.gov.

Various Writings
Brezhnev, Leonid. *Peace, Détente, Cooperation*. Translated. New York: Consultants Bureau, 1981.

Carter, Jimmy. *Keeping Faith – Memoirs of a President*. New York: Bantam Books, 1982.

Dobrynin, Anatoly. *In Confidence – Moscow's Ambassador to Six Cold War Presidents (1962-1986)*. New York: Times Books, 1995.

Dobrynin, Anatoly. Foreword to *Soviet-American Relations: The Détente Years, 1969-1972*. Washington, D.C.: United States Government Printing Office, 2007.

Ford, Gerald. *A Time to Heal*. New York: Harper & Row, Publishers, 1979.

Gromyko, Andrei. *Memoirs*. Translated by Harold Shukman. New York: Doubleday, 1989.

Kissinger, Henry. *Crisis – The Anatomy of Two Major Foreign Policy Crises*. New York: Simon & Schuster, 2003.

Kissinger, Henry. *Diplomacy*. New York: Simon & Schuster, 1994.

Kissinger, Henry. Foreword to *Soviet-American Relations: The Détente Years, 1969-1972*. Washington, D.C.: United States Government Printing Office, 2007.

Kissinger, Henry. *White House Years*. New York: Simon & Schuster, 1979.

Kissinger, Henry. *Years of Upheaval*. New York: Simon & Schuster, 1982.

Kissinger, Henry. *Years of Renewal*. New York: Simon & Schuster, 1999.

Nixon, Richard. *RN – The Memoirs of Richard Nixon*. New York: Grosset & Dunlap, 1978.

Sakharov, Andrei. "A Letter to the Congress of the United States." In *Sakharov Speaks*, ed. Harrison E. Salisbury, 212-215. New York: Alfred A. Knopf, 1974.

Solzhenitsyn, Aleksandr. "America: You Must Think About the World." June 30, 1975. In *Détente – Prospects for Democracy and Dictatorship*, 7-38. New Brunswick, New Jersey: Transaction Books, 1976.

Video Recordings
Frost/Nixon – The Complete Interviews. 400 minutes. Paradine Television Inc., 1977. DVD.

Nixon. Produced by David Espar, Elizabeth Deane, and Marilyn Mellowes. 170 minutes. WGBH Educational Foundation, 1990. DVD.

Reagan. Produced by Adriana Bosch and Austin Hoyt. 253 minutes. WGBH Educational Foundation, 1998. DVD.

Index